D0396270

UNLEASH YOUR GREATNESS

BECOME A PERSON OF IMPACT

By
Rick Olson & Robert J. Strand

Published by Ross Publishing
Dallas, WI 54733

Every effort has been made to contact the authors or originators of the stories contained in this book. Most are a result of conversations, while others were accumulated throughout the course of a thirty-year radio and television broadcasting career.

Printed in the United States of America

Ross Publishing Company
PO Box 27
Dallas, WI 54733
Tel: (715)837-1288   Fax: (715)837-1220

Ordering information
Special discounts are available on quantity purchases by corporations, associations, and others. For details, contact Ross Publishing at the address above, or visit www.rickolsonseminars.com

Library of Congress Control Number 2002090671

ISBN 0-9718512-0-4
First paperback printing March 2002
Second paperback printing December 2004

Editing: Tracey Finck
Cover design: Bolger Concept To Print/Jim Weinberg
Printed by: Bolger Concept To Print

Dedication

If you combined a truckload of love and affirmation, unswerving faith and encouragement, and the relentless pursuit of a goal, you would have Lori Olson, my wife and the joy of my life. She was my number one cheerleader during the lean, early years of my public speaking. She had the vision for this book and the patience to see it through to completion.

This book is also dedicated to my three children:

Thad – whose immense talents are outstripped only by his great people skills.
Kelsi – a fantastic student who is about to make the world a much better place.
Seth – who has the magical ability to put a smile on the face of everyone he meets.

–Rick Olson

To the next generation of *motivators*, my eight grandkids: Christopher, Kristie, Sarah, Cody, Casey, Jonathan, Benjamin and Maxwell. They really don't have a choice to be anything but motivated because their parents have built an inner fire within them.

–Robert J. Strand

Contents

Acknowledgements

Some very special people took our manuscript, read and reread every word, and gave us wonderful suggestions and insights. Heartfelt thanks to: Juline Albert, Tracey Finck, Dorothy Groshong, Marge Gunhus, Marilu Hoferman, and Pama Olson.

Introduction

If you live with the tension between what is and what could be, and if you would like to scream out "Status Quo - It Must Go!" you are a prime candidate to create a preferred future. This book is written to unlock key concepts that can take the boundaries off your future.

The way you think has everything to do with the impact your life has on the people around you. In this book, you will be challenged to think new thoughts about your attitude, the way you communicate, and how you plan.

This book is designed to help remove boundaries you may have placed on your own impact and effectiveness. So, how should this book be read? S - L - 0 - W - L - Y. As Francis Bacon said, "Some books are to be tasted, others to be swallowed, and some few to be chewed and digested." Plan to chew on this one for quite some time. It has been written with several bite sized chapters, each focusing on a fresh concept, so that it can be read, thought about, and integrated and implemented into your life. Each chapter has three parts: There are quotes related to each theme. The quotes are original quotations by the two authors (RJO - Rick Olson or RJS - Robert Strand). The first page of each chapter is written by Rick Olson with the purpose of teaching a concept. The second page of each chapter is written by Robert Strand with the purpose of illustrating or giving an application of the teaching.

Ideally, each chapter should be read and applied before moving on. Take a week or more to work on the new concept, then go on to the next one. A key thought to remember: it takes 21 days to develop a new habit.

Here is the good news. One chapter of your life is already written. A new chapter is about to be written. With some bold, new thinking, it could be a best seller.

Turn The Keys To Success!

By Robert J. Strand

What really is *success*? You will soon discover that there are about as many definitions of success as there are people who write about success! In its broadest definition, to "succeed" at anything is to "be fruitful, be effective, do well, bear fruit, click, hit, catch, attain a goal, achieve one's aim, to be triumphant, avail, win, prosper, make good, find fulfillment, move up, come into possession of, have a happy outcome, to advance, to be completed, thriving, and well-received!" Wow!

Did you notice one thing? Not once did I spell success like this: "$ucce$$!" To define success in terms of money only is to find the very narrowest of meanings. Success may well mean more money to you, but not necessarily so.

One of the best definitions of success is from Samuel J. Moore, founder of "Moore Business Forms, Inc." It goes like this: "Success is to have done that which has benefited the largest number of people and which, when you have finished your work, has left the world better because you have lived in it."

Now, in order to best get across the point I'm about to write, I wish I could be like that very creative salesman who managed to cross a carrier pigeon with a woodpecker. The offspring not only carried the message, they also knocked on doors.

This book has been written about successful concepts for making your business or personal life more productive, more successful. But simply knowing the concepts will not get the job done. Let's take a look at some life principles which will help you really get with it. Hopefully, these will move you from knowledge into action. So...here goes!

Key #1...APPLICATION:

Webster says that "application" is "anything applied as a remedy, a continued exertion." Continued exertion will get us just about anything we really want. It's simply another way of saying you must keep at the task, you must persevere. Robert Schuller writes: "Inch by inch, anything is a cinch!"

Lack of application is a problem with horses as well as with people. Eddie Arcaro, one of the greatest jockeys of all time, believed that ninety percent of the horses he rode took it easy, didn't put out to their maximum. His success as a jockey was a result of getting out of his rides more of what they were capable of doing. Wouldn't it be great if each of us had an Eddie Arcaro on our back to help us live to the maximum?

Charles Schwab, who ran the Carnegie Steel Empire and was reputed to be the first American to draw $1 million per year as salary, had a man named Ivey Lee come into his office one day. Mr. Lee told Mr. Schwab he would give him an idea that would save him more time and produce more results for him than any idea he'd been given. Lee said he wouldn't attempt to sell this idea but would allow him to use it for two weeks with the understanding that Mr. Schwab would pay him whatever he felt it was worth. After using this idea for two weeks, Mr. Schwab paid $25,000 to Ivey Lee.

So…what is this $25,000 idea? You're getting the use of it for the price of purchase of this book. Here it is: *Each morning, make a list of all the important things that you need to do during this day, listing the most important at the top. Always list more than you expect to accomplish on this particular day. The next morning, make a new list, referring to yesterday's unfinished list. Make another list…with the most important at the top and continue on through the week.* Simplicity itself. This idea will work for anyone who is willing to understand that nothing will work unless you do.

Got time for another Charles Schwab anecdote? One day Mr. Schwab received a telegram from one of his salesmen telling him that he had just sold the largest single order for steel in the in the history of the company. Mr. Schwab wired back: "WONDERFUL! What have you done today?"

One of the reasons why people don't use their time wisely is that they don't really know what their time is worth. For example, if your annual salary is $50,000, each of your work hours is worth $25.62, each minute $.4268 and if you managed to save one hour per day for a year, you would have $6,250.00! If your salary is $100,000 per year, just double the figures above. Understand that these figures are based upon 244 work days of eight hours each. This does include coffee breaks. (Consider this: Two coffee breaks a day of fifteen minutes each amounts

viii

to seventy-two hours per year which is nine full work days, plus the cost of coffee.)

Another form of application is found in work itself. John R. McCall, in a speech given to the National Meeting of the "Million Dollar Round Table" members, outlined four central desires of most people that correspond to the stages in a person's development: "*First*, there is the desire for pleasure which is predominant in a child and grows less and less important with advancing years. *Second*, there is the desire for success which can drive a person through early adulthood and produce great works, only to discover that success alone doesn't satisfy. The *third* desire which takes over is the desire to do one's duty even at the cost of pleasure and even sometimes to the lessening of financial success. The *last* and culminating desire is to understand, to find philosophical or religious meaning for one's own existence and for the existence of this world. To seek something that is worth dying for so we may have something worth living for. To seek a matrix of values that is our very own."

McCall went on to say that most really successful people reflect the third or fourth stages. "But, unfortunately, the majority of people never make it out of the first stage." Will Rogers was fond of saying: "Plans get you into things but you've got to work your way out!"

The concept that so many people never seem to understand is that the only place "success" comes before "work" is in the dictionary! And there are more people who die of worry than of work because more people are willing to worry than are willing to work. Once, while visiting in the home of a friend who was quite a practical joker, I picked up a book titled *How To Be a Success Without Working!* Hurriedly, I began to examine it, seeking to find the secret. You can well imagine my disappointment to find that every page in it was completely blank!

People have been searching for the "secret" to instant success almost from the beginning of time. We've developed computers that cycle in nano-seconds, airplanes that can fly faster than the speed of sound, rockets that can boost humans into space orbit and to the moon, but still no formulas for instant success! The American Motivational

Association has a slogan: "The elevator to success is out of order. You'll have to use the stairs, one step at a time." Remember also that "triumph" is nothing more than "try" added to "umph!" So we're back to where we started. In order to be a success at anything in life, you must apply yourself with perseverance.

Key #2...ENTHUSIASM:

Let's begin with a definition of this exciting concept. Webster says "enthusiasm" is: "intense or eager interest, zeal." But it's much more than that. Break the word down into its root meaning and we have something more. "Enthusiasm" comes from two Greek words..."en" and "theos," which literally translates: "God within!"

It is one of the most fascinating and misunderstood words in the English language. Almost everybody is for enthusiasm—sort of like motherhood, cherry pie, and the American flag. Everybody has the capacity to be enthused. Our inner capabilities are much the same because they are an inside emotion which works its way out.

Also, you must know that enthusiasm really has nothing to do with making lots of noise. Most of us aren't ready to jump up and down and shout. But likewise, your lack of outward noise or emotion doesn't mean you aren't getting stirred up. Animation and enthusiasm are not the same thing. But if you are animated, your actions can trigger enthusiasm. Dale Carnegie had a lot to say about this concept. For example: "If you want your audience to cry, you have to cry the first bucketful." So it is with making enthusiasm something that others can catch.

Here's one simple example of how enthusiasm for a product has skyrocketed the demand. When a chicken lays an egg, which usually is an all day job, she cackles and excitedly announces to the world in her most excited fashion that she has produced another! On the other hand, when a duck lays an egg, she is passive about the whole process. She just squats, grunts, and that's about all. Now all of us know that the demand for chicken eggs over duck eggs is much higher—in spite of the fact that a duck egg is about three times larger than a chicken egg.

How is it possible to become more enthusiastic? Percy Whiting says there are two ways: "Pep talks and faith talks." A pep talk is a short pepper-upper, a light-hearted, get-with-it kind of thing. We see it used often by sales managers and in the sports world. But it's also the kind of message you can give yourself on a daily basis. It's best delivered in an animated vocal, rapid fire fashion. The amazing thing is that you don't even have to believe what you are telling yourself. It helps if you do, but by repetition you will soon convince yourself. *Why* does this work? The subconscious mind doesn't distinguish between the real and the imagined. When you give yourself or others this pep talk, you are planting concepts into the subconscious mind. This kind of a talk is designed for the short haul. It can give you a daily lift, which we all need. The "faith" talk is for something different. The best description of faith is from the Bible, *"Faith is belief in things not yet seen."* This kind of a talk is delivered in a very serious fashion. This is the time to count your blessings and give yourself the assurance that you can reach your life goals.

As your new-found enthusiasm builds, you will be as confident of your newly found asset as the fellow who sat around the house every night whiling away his time by constantly playing only one note on his cello. His wife had never seen nor heard anybody but her husband play the cello, so she finally convinced him to take her to a symphony concert. As the music was about to begin, she excitedly pointed out the six cello players and that all of them were running their fingers and bows up and down the strings, playing lots of different notes. He, with a great deal of confident pride, replied, "Oh, they're all just looking for the note I've found."

Key #3...ESTABLISH REALISTIC GOALS:

Ben Franklin once said, "If you would not be forgotten, either write things worth reading or do things worth writing about." Your thoughts about your future are very important because you are going to spend the rest of your life there. Nobody plans failure, particularly not a twenty-five-year old. Insurance industry statistics let us look ahead forty years into the future and see what will happen to one hundred people who are now age twenty-five: Of these one hundred, one will be wealthy;

four will be comfortable and have all the money they need to live on and retire on; five will still be working in order to live; thirty-six will have died; and fifty-four will be dependent upon family, friends or some government agency for their retirement livelihood!

Why? Fewer than five percent of these people had clearly defined goals! The other ninety-five percent followed any path marked, If you don't know where you're going, any road will take you there.

Napoleon put it another way: "Circumstance...I make my circumstance!" Yes. You, too, must decide to make your circumstance by deciding to have, write, and then to live by your goals.

Chris Hegarty, a management consultant and sales trainer from Tiburon, California tells us of a study made by Yale University of some of their graduates who had been out of the university for twenty years: three percent of these graduates had taken time to write down their life goals; ten percent had talked in broad terms about what they wanted to do with their lives; eighty-seven percent had not bothered to write down goals and hadn't even given much thought to them. They found that the result of twenty years showed that the three percent had achieved more material, more professional success than the other ninety-seven percent combined! To see the moral of this story doesn't require a Ph.D. in statistical analysis.

Writing down your goals is the place to start! Do it now! Don't put it off because it may be the most important thing you can do with your life. If you have achieved your goals, then make it your goal to find another goal!

Ben Franklin said, "Living without a goal is like shooting without a target!" Along with this, there is an ancient Chinese Proverb: "Hungry men sit long time in chair with mouth open waiting for roast duck to fly in."

Florence Chadwick, the San Diego-born distance swimmer, was the first woman to swim the English Channel in both directions. On her first attempt to swim the channel it was a foggy day and she gave up less than three miles short of the French coast. On her return to England, she said that if she could have seen the shores of France, she would have made it. On her second attempt it was a sunny, clear day and she made it!

xii

Let's recap some of the concepts in establishing goals: 1) Make up your mind to create a goal. 2) Write it out in detail. 3) Be specific. 4) Be obsessed about accomplishing your goal. 5) Make it difficult enough to reach so that you must extend yourself to attain it. 6) Check often on your progress. 7) If possible, always keep your goal in sight. 8) As soon as you reach that goal, repeat this process as you move on to the next goal.

Key #4...ATTITUDE:

To my way of thinking, attitude is the most important of these four keys. The astonishing thing about this concept is that you can't change any attitudes but your own. Nobody can give you a good attitude or a better attitude. All that I or anybody else can do is to make you aware by example or written word what attitude is all about. Then, too, we must remember that it's easier to create a new attitude than it is to change an established attitude.

Cavett Robert zeroes in on the problem through what he calls "the law of emotional gravity." He says, "One pessimist can pull four optimists down much quicker than four optimists can pull one pessimist up."

A good self-image is the starting place from which to build a good attitude. If you do not like you...who will? I'm not talking about vain pride, but a positive sense about who you really are. I like what Ethel Waters once said: "God didn't make no junk!"

You see, in the bottom line, it's simply that success comes in "cans" and failure comes in "can'ts." Everywhere we look, the importance of the "I can" attitude is shouted to us. You do not need to look any further than to the name of our country. What are we? We are Americans! It's not "Amer-I-can't!" It's "Amer-I-CAN!"

There has probably been more written about this subject than any other when it comes to motivational materials. Scholars have disagreed on a lot of things, but I believe I'm pretty safe saying that they all agree on the importance of this subject having to do with attitude in life.

Ralph Waldo Emerson said, "A man is what he thinks about all day long." William Shakespeare wrote, "Our doubts are traitors and make us lose the good we oft might win by fearing to attempt." William James, the father of modern psychology often said, "The greatest discovery of my generation is that human beings can alter their lives by altering their attitudes of mind."

Jack Dempsey, former world heavy-weight boxing champion, was once approached by a small antagonist who told him, "If I were as big as you I would go out into the woods and get me the biggest bear I could find and tear him limb from limb."

Dempsey replied, "Oh, yeah? There are a lot of little bears out there in those woods, too." Yes, there are lots of experts who are more than willing to tell you what your attitude should be rather than doing something about their own.

Vince Lombardi was one of the greatest developers of the positive mental attitude in others while coaching the Green Bay Packers. He once said, "Unless a man believes in himself, makes a total commitment to his career and puts everything he has into it, he will never be successful at anything he undertakes." He was so committed to this ideal that he was more than once accused of not having ulcers but of being a carrier.

Then, there is another old Chinese proverb: "Man who say it cannot be done should not interrupt man doing it!"

Your successes in life will truly be dependent upon what you can get out of yourself! Your attempts to improve your attitude are going to require effort and sacrifice.

When I hear the word "sacrifice" I think of the old story about the chicken and pig that were walking off the desert into a small town. There, hanging across the street, in front of the only restaurant in town, was a sign proclaiming: "Ham and eggs, The All-American breakfast." They stopped and looked, then the chicken said to the pig, "Doesn't that sign make you proud?" After a moment's thought the pig replied, "That's easy for you chickens to say. All that requires from you is a daily commitment...but for us pigs that is a total sacrifice!"

Whether you just have a small commitment or make a total sacrifice, it will be worth the effort because success, in the bottom line, after all, is a journey as well as a destination! Turn these four keys and begin your walk through the doorway to success!

xiv

WHICH AM I?

I watched them tearing a building down
A gang of men in a busy town,
With a ho-heave and lusty yell
They swung a beam and a side wall fell;
I asked the foreman, "Are these men skilled
And the men you'd hire if you had to build?"
He gave a laugh and said, "No, indeed!
Just common labor is all I need;
I can easily wreck in a day or two what
Builders have taken a year to do!"
And I thought to myself as I went away,
"Which of these roles have I tried to play?"

Am I a builder who works with care, measuring
Life by the rule and square?
Am I shaping my deed to well made plan,
Patiently doing the best I can?
Or am I a wrecker, who walks the town,
Content with the labor of tearing it down?
(Author is unknown)

Say Goodbye To A Boring Life

By Rick Olson

If you were to select a group of words that best describes your life right now, which words would you reach for?

- Significant, adventurous, action-filled, cutting edge, adrenaline rush, new, fresh, exciting, challenging, rewarding, fulfilling, stimulating.
- Sameness, routine, dull, boring, existing, hanging on, functioning, coping.

Someone once said, "The trouble with life is, you are halfway through before you realize it is one of those do-it-yourself deals." If your life has settled into just existing, perhaps it is time to quit waiting for your life to happen. Start making it happen. When were you last tied into some project that woke you up in the middle of the night and forced you to the dining room table where you wrote fast and furiously as thoughts came to you? When did you last pull the car off the road because you were so excited about your thoughts that you had to capture them on paper? When did you last do something that was bigger than you were; it impacted lots of people and it made a tremendous difference in the lives of others?

If your life continues on the very same course that you are on right now, will you be satisfied with what is eventually put on your tombstone? Are there dreams that you have tossed around but for some reason have never acted upon? Do you spend your life looking at events around you and saying, "Someone ought to do something about that." Or, do you look at your surroundings and say, "I'm going to do something about that." This one thing characterizes people of impact: they do things that others refuse to do. What is it that holds others back? Sometimes it is fear, sometimes it is lack of courage, and sometimes it is laziness. But, people who do significant things with their lives fight through these hurdles to impact the world in which they live.

It is time to view yourself in a different light. It is time to view yourself as a difference-maker, a change agent. Perhaps others have seen you as a philosopher and a dreamer. It is time to change their thinking. It is time to become known for having a bias for action.

Had we lived in another time we might have had the joy of working closely with a large group of people to build a barn or design a beautiful quilt. But, barn raisings and quilting bees, for most, are a thing of the past. Today, most people don't have the joy of working with a group of people and accomplishing a great task, unless a natural disaster strikes. At that time the hero seems to come out in most people. But, without a natural disaster, most people have to look many years into their past to think of the last time they gave their efforts to a project or cause that made a difference for others. In the chapters that follow, thirty-four ideas are shared on how you can be a difference maker. Specific insights are given on how to become a person of impact. Accumulation of things will never satisfy the burning desire within to do something of significance in your life. Rather, it is in the giving of your talents and energy that life takes on meaning and you discover joys that purchasing products could never offer.

My motto is simply this: Giving is living! I wrote it in my Bible years ago and strive to live it out in my personal life, my business life, and my spiritual life. The following are some events that I have had the privilege of being involved in in recent years. These events have brought a great sense of joy and fulfillment to my life.

In 1993, I was living in Elk River, Minnesota. I challenged a group of leaders in our community to volunteer their time and effort and together build a house in seven days. Our goal was to then sell the house on the open market and give all the proceeds to the DARE Program. That bold plan captivated the community. Eventually, over 200 companies made donations and 300 individuals volunteered their time. The house was actually completed in just six days. The project received state and national publicity. Our original goal was to raise $50,000. We went $68,000 beyond that goal and raised $118,000. It impacted the psyche of every person involved in a way that nothing else ever had. People felt great about themselves, about their community, and it seemed to usher in a new can-do spirit in the city of Elk River. I am convinced that at the end of my life I will still look back on that week as one of my favorites.

I have been closely tied in to many charities. They all have one thing in common; they need money. For several charities, I have coordinated an effort where we have encouraged diehard golfers to volunteer their time and play 100 holes of golf in one day to raise money for charity. Each golfer is challenged to raise pledge support per hole. These fundraisers have netted from $10,000 - $40,000. At the end of the day lots of weary golfers leave the course knowing they have made a world of difference for a great cause.

I have conducted a number of retreats for the top Realtors in the Midwest. At these retreats, we have sold the top-producing Realtors to other realtors who desired to shadow them for one day doing business their way. The idea is they get to follow them for one day, see how they spend their time, and learn every insight they can. Several Realtors have paid up to $1,000 dollars for the privilege of watching a top-flight Realtor for a day. Those dollars were given to charity. In total, we have raised $25,000 for some outstanding charities.

The church that I attend is small in number, about 150 in attendance on Sunday morning. Our congregation wanted to give a gift to our community. We put together an event called "Christmas Tree Lane." We took advantage of our large, visible parking lot and placed ten beautiful, colorful Christmas scenes around the parking lot. This event involved over one hundred of our people. And it has brought great joy to the community as nearly 2,000 people per year have driven through our Christmas Tree Lane.

You are surrounded by unsolved problems. Every one of those problems represents a tremendous opportunity for you to become a person of impact and an invaluable member of your community. Here are vital steps to becoming a person of impact:
- Really see what is going on around you.
- Don't just look at the obvious.
- Ask great questions.
- Discover the pain.
- Find out what isn't working.
- Lock into your surroundings and see what needs your help.
- Make a commitment to do something.

It takes a bias for action. It takes a commitment to going beyond the dreaming stage. Don't allow yourself to say, "Somebody ought to do something about that." Rather, state the words that make all the difference in the world, "Something needs to be done; I'm going to do something about it!"

Devise a bold plan. Small plans captivate no one. They do not have the ability to stir people's blood. But bold plans captivate people. They make them lean forward. They stir up the curiosity within each person. That is why people responded so well to the challenge of building a house in seven days. It is what inspires every diehard golfer to say, "I would love to play 100 holes of golf in a day." In every case, the cause was noble, the plans were bold, and people responded.

Understand that people support what they create. A surefire recipe for disaster is this: go to a solitary place, design the entire plan, bring it back to the masses, and try to get a buy in. More than likely, you will be left twisting in the wind. The reason is simple. If people have no say in birthing the idea they have no emotional attachment to it. It is possible to get the finest energy from many if you will simply allow them to help create the plan.

Know what finished work looks like. It is perseverance and not talent that rules supreme. Talented failures are a dime a dozen. It is the ability to keep going after the other person quits that makes all the difference. Stick with your plan and your project all the way through to completion. Finishers are a rare species. Initiators are a dime a dozen. Take the idea all the way to the finish line.

It is time to cut loose. Adventure is just around the bend. Once you taste the action of the playing field, you will never again be content to sit in the bleachers!

UNLEASH YOUR GREATNESS

BECOME A PERSON OF IMPACT

Don't waste energy worrying
about how people feel about you.
Assume they like you!
~RJO~

1

Assume People Like You

How do you feel when you meet someone for the first time? Expectant and confident? Or, do you feel nervous, worrying about how you look, what you are going to say, and how you are going to come across to that new person? The new people you meet have everything to do with the quality of your life and the possibilities ahead. You can't afford to come across as nervous. Try this on for size. Next time you meet a new person, assume he or she likes you! That's right. Not one second wasted worrying about yourself. Assume they like you, treat them as if they do, and make it impossible for them to not. In so doing, you will be able to focus all your energy on them. You can give them the best you have if you are not worried about yourself. If you don't assume they like you, you will waste much of your energy focusing on yourself. You will be worrying about how you look and how you come across. Your concern will be about you and not about them. That removes all of the dynamic possibilities from the encounter. Take yourself out of the equation. Imagine that people are "crazy" about you. Now you can direct 100 percent of your energy toward them.

Assuming that they like you will help you develop a host mentality. If you wait on people to notice you and serve you, you will spend your whole life being disappointed. Instead, do the things a good host does; greet people, anticipate and meet their needs, make them feel at home. You will never lack for friends or customers. Assuming that they like you will open many new and exciting doors. You will not be hesitant to meet anyone. You will develop relationships with dynamic people, people who think big. Get ready to expand your life a great deal. Get ready to impact people in ways you haven't in the past. And get ready to be impacted by people who are making a mark in the world.

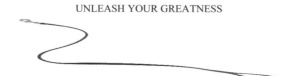

Friendly Faces
And Friendly Places

A farmer was out working in his field near the road when along came a very tired-looking, obviously weary man who was shuffling up the road. "Where are you headed, friend?" the friendly farmer called out.

The startled man looked up with a frown and answered the farmer: "I'm headed to the next town. What are the people like in the next town?"

"What were the people like in the town you just left?" asked the farmer.

"They were rude and unkind. I sure was glad when it came time to leave them behind," the weary man replied.

Then the farmer answered: "I am sorry to have to tell you this, but the people in the next town are going to be rude and unkind like the last town."

The next day, the farmer was again working in his field by the same road when he noticed another man coming down the road toward him. "Where are you headed, friend?" the farmer called out.

The man smiled, greeted the farmer and said, "I'm headed to the next town up the road. By the way, what are the people like in this town?"

"What were the people like in the town you just left?" The farmer asked. "Oh, they were wonderful people. They were friendly, kind, and everyone seemed to like me. They really made me feel welcome. I was really sorry when I had to leave them," the man answered.

The farmer smiled and replied, "I am delighted to inform you that the people in this next town are going to like you and will be just like the people of your last town."

Interesting how different the same town can be within one day!

The happy person chooses
a right attitude and is not
dependent on right
circumstances.
~RJS~

Statements tend to push people
away from you.
Questions always pull people
towards you.
~RJO~

2

Your Ears Make You Money

What will make you more money, your mouth or your ears? We all want to be good with words. We would love to tell a clever story, have a great one-liner, or be as persuasive as a "dream-team" lawyer. Few of us are. Here is the great news. Your ears have the potential of making you the most money. You do not have to be eloquent to be very effective in sales or customer service. When you talk too much you push people away from you. When you ask good questions, you always pull people towards you. You become more interesting, more caring, and increase your chances of really connecting with the other person as you focus on them by really listening.

Are you a true listener, or one who merely waits for your turn to talk? Most people seem to be plagued by autobiographical listening. That strong urge to talk and keep yourself in the spotlight may feed your ego, but it will drive people from you. And that will cost you a lot of money. The most effective salespeople have realized that to be effective, they should talk about thirty percent of the time, and listen seventy percent of the time. The reason is quite simple: your statements tend to push people away from you, while questions have a way of pulling people towards you. Notice how long you listen to a rambling bore before you are looking for the exit door. Conversely, you are willing to pay a psychologist top dollar, even though they often don't talk a lot. The combination of dynamic listening and insightful questions cause them to be very effective, not to mention wealthy. The pressure is off. You don't have to be clever, but you do have to listen well.

Handwriting On The Wall

A weary mother returned from her shopping trip to the store.
Lugging groceries through the kitchen door.
Awaiting her arrival was her eight-year-old-son,
Anxious to relate what his younger brother had done.
"While I was out playing and Dad was on a call,
T.J. took his crayons and wrote on the wall!
It's on the new paper you hung in the den.
I told him you'd be mad at having to do it again."
She let out a moan and furrowed her brow,
"Where is your little brother right now?"
She emptied her arms and with a purposeful stride,
She marched to his closet where he had gone to hide.
She called his name as she entered his room.
He trembled with fear...he knew that meant doom!
For the next ten minutes, she ranted and raved
About the expensive wallpaper and how she had saved.
Lamenting all the work it would take to repair,
She condemned his actions and total lack of care.
The more she scolded, the madder she got,
She stomped from his room, totally distraught!
She headed for the den to confirm her fears,
When she saw the wall, her eyes flooded with tears.
The message she read pierced her soul with a dart,
It said, "I love Mommy," surrounded by a heart.
Well...the wallpaper remained, just as she found it,
With an empty picture frame hung to surround it.
A reminder to her, and indeed to all,
Take time to listen and read and to check
the handwriting on the wall.
(Author is unknown...adapted)

Real communication doesn't
begin with being understood
but with listening until you
understand others.
~RJS~

Until you attach a deadline to it, that goal is nothing more than a dream.

~RJO~

3

A Goal Is A Dream With A Deadline

Everyone has a dream. Some have the uncanny ability to turn their dream into reality, while others spend much of their life wishing they would get their big break and see their dreams come true. What is it that moves a dream past the dream stage and into reality? One thing makes all the difference. A deadline. Until there is a deadline, it remains wishful thinking. A deadline will stir creativity, sharpen your focus, and summon your resourcefulness.

When you were a child, life was easy. Mom or dad continually gave you deadlines. You knew when to get up. You knew when to make your bed, when to brush your teeth, when to pick up your toys, when to do your homework. Deadlines were attached to everything you did. It was the same in school. Now you are on your own. If you are going to be a high achiever, you must set self-imposed deadlines.

In 1953, a study was conducted on the graduating class of Yale University. Among the questions asked was, "Do you have written goals for your life?" Only three percent of that class of high achievers said yes. Twenty years later, when they did a follow-up study on the same class, they discovered that the three percent who had written goals for their life, now owned ninety-seven percent of the wealth in the class of '53.

Take the dream; attach a realistic deadline to it. Then back up and break down the project into bite-size pieces. Then attach deadlines to each. You have just mapped out a formula for success, a roadmap for the future. You have moved from uncertainty to clear focus. You are well on your way toward achievement.

The Hottest Week In July

Stanley Arnold, who became known for his million-dollar ideas, started in retail. His father opened Cleveland's first supermarket in 1937, which expanded into a chain of fifteen "Pick-N-Pay" stores. Stanley Arnold had the first of his "million-dollar" marketing ideas in one of those stores. As he sat in one of the fifteen empty stores in the snow-bound city, plans for an unprecedented retailing event began to take shape in his fertile brain. He asked all of his able-bodied employees to report to work the following day. When they did, Arnold asked them to make large snowballs in the parking lots. That day, thousands of snowballs were packed into grapefruit crates, eighty to a box, which were then taken to a deep freeze facility where Arnold had arranged for the snowballs to be kept at twenty degrees below zero for a definite period.

Everybody thought that the boss's brain had been frostbitten. Meanwhile, he was busy finding out from the weather bureau when the year's worst heat wave was most likely to occur. It was the 15th of July! Armed with this information, he proposed a joint promotional sale of General Food's Birdseye Frozen products. This sale was to be held the hottest week of July and would be called "A Blizzard of Values," along with an array of prizes and giveaways.

Summer came and for once the forecasters hit it right. In the 100 degree heat, special contingents of Cleveland's finest had to hold back hysterical women in the parking lots to keep them from mobbing the already crowded stores. During five days of "Pick-N-Pay's Blizzard of Values" more than 40,000 General Foods samples were given away, along with thousands of grapefruit-sized snowballs! It was a huge success!

Stanley Arnold concluded: "Thousands of customers had a good time and the food industry began to take notice of the great potential of excitement and deadlines as ingredients in selling!"

12

Achievers set goals;
losers create excuses!
~RJS~

If you want to be more than a spectator, get out of the bleachers.

~RJO~

4

Get Out Of The Bleachers

I have been on the playing field and I have sat in the bleachers. There is no comparison. The greatest thrills are found on the playing field. Much of life is missed when we find ourselves saying, "Somebody ought to do something about that." Three things usually happen. First, our friends and neighbors are saying the same thing, so nothing is really happening. Second, we miss out on the thrill of helping to solve a problem. Third, we miss out on the creative spin-offs that take place when we roll up our sleeves and get involved with other people. Why is it that we often think someone else is more qualified to handle the situation or capitalize on the opportunity? It is common to overestimate the abilities of others and underestimate our own abilities. When we arrive at a healthy state, we have a healthy respect for the abilities of others, while nurturing a growing confidence that says, "I can do that!"

It has been said that problems are opportunities in work clothes. Take a good look at what could be done. What could you do to make a difference? The question that should be asked every time you face a problem or opportunity should be, *what if?* Ask it often. Look at it from every angle. Check it out from every side. What if we did this? Your energy and insights could make all the difference!

Are things merely happening around you, or are you making things happen? A life lived to the full is much closer than you think. Commit to making things happen by getting out of the bleachers and getting on to the playing field. Remove once and forever the phrase from your vocabulary, "Somebody ought to do something about that."

"Just Do It"

It was Monday night, August 3rd at the 1992 Olympics in Barcelona, Spain. At the track and field stadium the gun sounded for the 400-meter semi-finals. About 100 meters into the race, Britain's Derek Redmond crumpled to the track with a torn right hamstring. Medical attendants rushed to assist him but as they approached Redmond, he waved them all aside, struggled to his feet, fell down, crawled, and hopped in a desperate effort to finish the race.

Four years earlier, he had qualified for the 1988 Olympics in Seoul, Korea. Ninety seconds before his heat, he had to pull out of the competition because of an "Achilles" tendon problem. Following this injury, he had five surgeries. Yet somehow he qualified again for this 1992 Olympics.

Now he'd just suffered a career-ending injury, however with a determined look on his face he thought, "I'm not quitting! Somehow I will finish this race!" Painfully, he worked his way down his lane toward the goal.

Up in the stands, a huge guy wearing a T-shirt, tennis shoes, and a "JUST DO IT" Nike cap, barreled out of the stands, hurled aside a security guard, jumped the barrier, ran to Derek's side, and embraced him. He was Jim Redmond, Derek's father.

Jim was one of those sports dads who changed his whole life for the sake of his athlete child. Now, with the father's arm around the son's waist and the son's arm on the father's shoulder, together they continued.

The crowd was stunned and on its feet, applauding, crying, cheering, weeping. Derek and his dad worked their way around the track until finally, together, they crossed the finish line!

It's moving out of the stands and onto the field of action which allows another to cross the finish line...and you to reach the goal, too!

People may doubt
what you say,
but they will believe
what you do.
~RJS~

The most basic question
regarding leadership is this:
Is anyone following?
~RJO~

5

Leaders Know Where They're Going And Can Take Others With Them

What is it that attracts people to a leader? What would make someone want to follow the lead of someone else? One thing that must be present is clear direction.

Do others know where you are headed? Do those close to you understand the direction you are going? If it is a mystery to them, it will be impossible for them to follow you.

If you want to test your leadership effectiveness, one question will sum it all up. Will people follow me? If they will not, it could be that they don't know where you are leading them.

Leadership effectiveness requires that you know the direction you are headed and can find a way to effectively communicate that to others. Seventy-five percent of all problems in business stem from poor communication.

Is there anything more debilitating than NETMA (Nobody Ever Tells Me Anything)? When people are left in the dark, it is the breeding ground for gossip and unrest.

Meet with your team often, and communicate your vision clearly. It will keep everyone on the same sheet of music, it will help you to refocus, and it will insure that the vision remains alive.

Let's compare your vision to a picture. Although the vision is clear in your mind (a complete picture) those who look to you have a blank canvas. Your role as a leader is to recreate the vision on their canvas. Don't take shortcuts in the vision-sharing process or their picture will be incomplete. They may be willing to follow, but they must know where you are going.

Go And Do Thou Likewise

A favorite story of mine has to do with a newly hired traveling salesman who had just sent in his first sales report to the home office. It stunned the brass in the sales department because it was obvious that the new salesman was ignorant! At the very best...he couldn't spell. This is what he wrote in his report: "I seen this outfit which they ain't never bot a dim's worth of nothin from us and I sole them some goods. A couple hunred tousand. I'm now goin to Chicawgo."

Before the man could be given the heave-ho by the sales manager, along came this report from Chicago: "I cum hear and sole them a millyon and a haff."

Fearful if he did and afraid if he didn't fire the ignorant salesman, the sales manager dumped the problem into the lap of the company president. The following morning, the ivory-towered sales department members were amazed to see posted on the bulletin board the above two letters written by the ignorant salesman...but with this memo from the company President posted underneath: "We ben spendin two much time trying to spel instead of tryn to sel. Let's get with those sails. I want everybody should read these letters from Gooch who is out on the rode doin a grate job for us and you should go out and do like he don." (My computer spell check went crazy on the above.)

Obviously, anybody in leadership would much prefer to have salespersons who can spell as well as sell. However, there are many people who have produced great results who were not "qualified" in our eyes.

A good leader will take advantage of the situation and use influence rather than position to lead others to a higher performance level.

20

The most successful of
leaders find the best people
for real tasks and leave them
alone to do their jobs.
~RJS~

There are many things in life
that you have no control over.
Attitude is not one of them.
~RJO~

6

Your Attitude Is A Choice

Some people have lots of bad days; others have few. The determining factor is your attitude. Simply put, attitude is nothing more than a choice. Charles Swindoll says, "The longer I live, the more I realize the impact of attitude on life. Attitude, to me, is more important that facts, it is more important than the past, than education, than money, than circumstances, than failures, than successes, than what other people think or say or do....I am convinced that life is ten percent what happens to me, ninety percent how I react to it."

Bad stuff happens to everyone. No one is exempt. But it is not an excuse for having a bad attitude. It is not good enough to have a great attitude four out of five days. That is most pleasant for those who cross your path on one of those four days. What about the poor lost souls who happen to see you on day five? They are not aware that you have had a stellar week. All they know is that they picked the wrong day. Eventually, people begin to approach cautiously to see if it is safe or not. The true professional makes a choice to have a great attitude each day.

Not only does your attitude affect all those around you, it either gives great energy to your day or drains it away. If you show up with a great attitude, an eight-hour day will seem like four hours. And if you show up with a bad attitude, it will seem more like a twelve-hour day.

Dr. William Glaser had this to say about it: "The world is divided into two types of people, those who are happy, healthy, pleasant, and cheerful, and those who are unhappy, unhealthy, unpleasant, and sad. The difference is, people in the first group evaluate themselves and try to improve, while the second group evaluates others and blames." The key to your attitude is not out there somewhere. It is within.

Four Men With Problems

Imagine…four chairs placed in front of us. And into these four chairs let's seat four different men with four problems. One of these men can't talk, one can't walk, one cannot see, and the other can't hear. In spite of their physical limitations, the era in which they have lived, and other negative factors they lived with, each of these had one thing in common: the "I-can" attitude!

The **FIRST MAN** was born tongue-tied and couldn't speak so others could understand him. He vowed that he would make his tongue work properly because he had something special to say. He went out in the forest every day and practiced with pebbles in his mouth to make his tongue work. Then he went on to become one of the greatest of the Greek orators who literally changed the world. His name was DEMOSTHENES!

The **SECOND MAN** said, "Even though polio has put me in a wheel chair and braces so that I can't walk, I will do something great for this land of mine!" Did he succeed? He became Governor of New York and President of the United States four times. His name was FRANKLIN DELANO ROOSEVELT!

The **THIRD MAN** knew a special truth: "If I think I can, I can!" He knew that even though he was blind he could create beautiful word pictures in other people's minds. Did he? He wrote beautiful poems such as *"Paradise Lost"* and *"Paradise Regained."* His name was JOHN MILTON!

The **FOURTH MAN** had a fierce belief in himself and said, "Despite the fact that I am deaf, I will put sounds in the ears of my fellow-man which will live forever!" You, perhaps, in the last few days may have been inspired by one of his numerous compositions. His name was LUDWIG VON BEETHOVEN!

This, the greatest key to success, is something no one can give you: A GOOD ATTITUDE!

There is no way to stop the
person with the correct mental
attitude from achieving a
goal…but there is nothing
on earth which can help the
person with the wrong attitude
to achieve anything.
~RJS~

Sales effectiveness has everything to do with finding solutions to problems.
~RJO~

7

Rethink The Term "Sales"

What if there wasn't such a word as "sales"? To be effective in sales, it is imperative that you have the right frame of mind concerning the sales process. You must remove any stigma associated with the word "sales" and free yourself up to be effective.

So could we come up with another word for the sales process? Could we call it something that puts it in a very positive light?

If you think of the sales process as pushing products, you will have a very difficult time making the call, knocking on the door or asking for the meeting. Who wants to be pushy?

If, however, you view it in another light, you will enjoy picking up the phone. How about viewing sales this way: Effective sales is nothing more than being a professional problem solver. How about if that is the new view of sales: Sales is "Professional Problem Solving."

- Are there people who need what you have?
- Are there people whose lives will be better if you help them?
- Is there pain you can remove?
- Are there obstacles you can help people overcome?
- Are there dreams you can help people accomplish?

If so, then the correct way to view this is, they have a problem and you have the wherewithal to help them overcome their problem. Because you choose to approach them in the most positive way, it makes you a professional problem solver. In that light, you can feel great about spending large amounts of your energy solving their problems.

So move out with confidence. You are a professional problem solver, about to build some dreams, solve some problems.

Get The Order!

As Jeno Paulucci, founder of Chun King, Jeno's Inc., and a number of other enormously successful businesses, graduated to becoming a commissioned "salesman" for a grocery wholesaler, he invented new techniques. Rather than calling on individual stores and selling in small amounts, Paulucci convinced grocers to form cooperatives and buy from him at a discounted rate for very large bulk purchases.

Soon, Paulucci was making more money on commission than the company president was on salary. It was then time to move on. He became fascinated with hydroponics and bean sprouts, which led him to Chun King, a very unpromising canned food business. He later sold Chun King to R.J. Reynolds for $63 million.

However, in the early days of attempting to sell his strange concoction of Cantonese food mixed with his mother's Italian spices, Paulucci wanted the chief buyer of the national chain, Food Fair, to taste his creation.

Now, as Max Gunther tells it, "Paulucci pulled out a can opener and pried the lid off a can of chop suey vegetables. Lying right on top of the vegetables, hidden from the buyer's view by the raised can lid, was a cooked grasshopper. It was the kind of accident that can happen to any food processing company once in a while, even the biggest. Chun King's kitchens, though based in a Quonset hut, were in fact as clean as anybody else's. But Paulucci was strongly aware, as he gazed horrified at the grasshopper, that his company's grand image was in mortal danger."

"He hesitated for half a second. Then he picked up a spoon, smiled broadly and said: 'This looks so good that I'm going to take the first mouthful myself.' He ate the spoonful, including the grasshopper, with apparent relish!" Jeno Paulucci got the order!

No salesmanship here, just a "professional problem solver" in action!

Opportunity in the sales world
is a moving target—and the
larger the potential,
the more quickly it moves.
~RJS~

There may not be a finer form
of recognition than saying,
"I need your creativity."
~RJO~

8

People Support
What They Help Create

Is there a surefire formula for organizational disappointment? Unequivocally there is. To insure widespread disillusionment, simply take a few select folks (the brain trust) away for a planning retreat, formulate a comprehensive plan, come back and present it to frontline workers, then watch them treat it like a dirty diaper.

Why do they do that? Simply, they did not create it. They have no investment in it. They have no say. They did not have the joy of the birthing process; therefore, they have no emotional attachment to it.

Would you like to get buy-in from everyone? It is most important to remember that people support what they help create. High energy, released creativity, and unusual productivity will flow as they get their hands around the problem. Let everyone involved own the problem and help formulate the solution. They will amaze you with their ability to solve great problems and overcome insurmountable hurdles. Tom Peters had this to say about it: "Our number one failure in business is not tapping the creativity of our worker's potential."

Here is how one business approached a problem. They were in a very competitive environment and wanted to take customer service to the highest level. They invited their employees to make their best suggestions which were then implemented over the course of the next year. They had a remarkable year, and decided to have a banquet to celebrate. They created a very festive setting, highlighted by streamers hanging from the ceiling. At the end of each streamer was a placard with a customer improvement suggestion. Then there was the name of the employee who suggested that improvement. In all, there were eighty-four streamers hanging from the ceiling. Their service program was a runaway success — their staff gave birth to it!

The Peak Performance

"These people are doing the best work of their lives.   And I have no idea why.   None of us knows why," said George, who supervised a team of scientists and engineers at an aerospace company. Something special was happening in the office cubicles, conference rooms, and machine shops that people didn't know how to explain.

What had changed several thousand ordinary men and women, merely competent workers, into super-achievers?

We're talking about the Grumman Aerospace Corporation plant at Bethpage, Long Island, who had just been commissioned to design and build the "Lunar Excursion Module" (LEM), the first manned craft that would land on the moon for the Apollo 11 mission.

This was a technological challenge unlike any other the United States had ever taken on.   The lives of the astronauts and the prestige of our nation would depend on the LEM's success. Were the people doing the planning and execution of it all winners, standouts, or geniuses? No. Its success didn't depend only on the bright stars with the right stuff...but on middle-range people, production people, thousands of people who had been reasonably successful.   What happened to move them to the next level?

George, himself, was one of those people who was only going through the motions.   That was before the "project."   He said: "I've been a piece of furniture in my job for years." He paused and pointed to the moon in the night sky and continued: "People have been dreaming about going there for thousands of years. And *we're* going to do it. You want to know why we're doing so well? I've got a mission...something that matters to all of us.   We finally have something we can sink our teeth into and be proud of."

A "peak performance" begins with a collective commitment to a well understood mission.

32

People who are participants
in the creation stage of a project
will be the most enthusiastic
supporters at the execution stage.
~RJS~

What does change feel like?
It feels like being suspended in
midair — between trapeze bars.
~RJO~

9

Change Is Inevitable

Why do we find change so unsettling? It is not the first time we've encountered it. Yet it always seems to have that same paralyzing effect. What is it about change that immobilizes us?

Picture the trapeze artist who swings out across this vast expanse holding onto the bar. Another bar has been released on the other side and swings out in a great arc towards the artist. His goal is to transfer from one bar to the other. One problem: He must let go of the first bar before taking hold of the second. That is unsettling.

Unsettled is precisely what we feel when we go through a time of great change. It feels like being between bars. We don't have the security of the past because we had to let it go. It is the in-between time that we find unsettling. It is not that we are so in love with the past. It is not that we are so fearful of the future. It is the uncertainty of not knowing that makes it very challenging. And much of life is spent between trapeze bars.

To be invaluable, make a commitment to be a person who is adept at moving through change and can help others navigate through those uncharted waters. It calls for context reframing.

Context reframing is looking at a challenging issue from a different viewpoint and discovering the possibilities that are there. That approach was taught to us years ago through childhood stories like Rudolf the Red-nosed Reindeer. To all the other reindeer, Rudolf's bright nose was strange, and they ostracized him from the group. But Santa was resourceful and saw that it was the very thing that could guide them through a foggy night. Santa's perception changed everything!

Things are changing around you, but if you will look again, you will see new possibilities that others will miss.

Responding To Changing Lifestyles

In an article about some of the challenges which face leaders in a rapidly changing business environment, the *"Royal Bank Letter"* from Canada stated: "Someone once described management as 'a Chinese baseball game.' In this mythical sport, both the ball and the bases are in motion. As soon as the ball is hit, the defending players can pick up the base bags and move them to anywhere in fair territory. The batters never know in advance where they must run to be safe." What an apt metaphor for the nature of change in business today.

Al Neuharth, chairperson and CEO of the Gannett Company, was justifiably concerned about the changes taking place in the newspaper business. Afternoon daily papers such as *The Philadelphia Bulletin, The Cleveland Press,* and *The Minneapolis Star and Tribune,* had met their demise. Why? America's lifestyles were changing. Instead of reading the newspaper when they came home from work, the television set became their news source. Local papers found it increasingly difficult to deal with loss of readership, rising costs, and the fall off in advertising revenues.

Neuharth and his management team recognized that now "the bases were being moved." They made the choice to capitalize on new technologies and zeroed in on the public desire. They created a daily national newspaper...therefore, *USA TODAY* was created!

Maybe you've heard about the group of Amish who pulled up stakes from their settlement in the Midwest and moved to a remote area in Peru. When asked their reason for doing so, one of them responded, "We got tired of having to move our wagons to the side of the road to let the cars go by."

That was their response to the pressures of change. What about you?

The toughest thing to change
about change is our attitude
toward change.
~RJS~

A commitment to excellence
is healthy; a commitment to
perfection is neurotic.
~RJO~

10

A Commitment To Perfection Is Neurotic

A commitment to excellence is healthy; a commitment to perfection is neurotic. It is that very commitment to perfection that keeps us from effectively delegating to others. Our expectations carry with them an unspoken set of standards. We are convinced that no one else is capable of carrying out the task to meet those expectations. In our mind, the only safe course is to do it ourselves. What is the result? We are overworked, we are totally stressed, we are at the doorstep of burnout. Those around us remain aloof and uninvolved.

The answer? Delegate, delegate, delegate! Even if those who report to you are not perfect, it is their very imperfection that will give them something in common with you. Set your standards high, strive for excellence, but rid yourself of the nasty debilitating thoughts of perfection. A great guideline for delegation is this: If someone can do something eighty percent as well as you, you are wasting time if you do it yourself. Here are some top keys for effective delegation:

- You should prescribe the outcome, not the process
- You get what you inspect, not what you expect
- Short-range projects provide lots of energy
- Small teams are the most functional
- People support what they create
- Getting input from others is a great way to recognize them

There is no limit to what can be accomplished if no one cares who gets the credit. You are in a position to unleash greatness. Delegate (not just the unpleasant jobs), and watch what can be done.

People Delegation Takes Time

In his day, Andrew Carnegie was the wealthiest man in America. He was born in Scotland and came with his parents to America as a small boy. He was ambitious and as he grew up worked at a variety of odd jobs. He eventually ended up as president of the largest steel manufacturer in the United States. But that's not the point of this story.

At one time he had forty-three millionaires working for him. (In those days a millionaire was really rare. A million in his day would be equivalent to about twenty-five million today.)

A reporter once asked Mr. Carnegie how he had managed to hire forty-three millionaires. He responded with the fact that of the forty-three, none were millionaires when they had started working for him but had become millionaires as a result of working for him and his company.

The reporter asked how he had managed to develop these men into millionaires, and how had they managed to become so valuable to him.

Carnegie replied that people are developed in the same way that gold is mined. When gold is mined, several tons of dirt is excavated and sifted in order to uncover an ounce of gold. But the miner goes into the mine looking for gold, not dirt. Carnegie said that when dealing with people, he looks for the gold, and then tests each discovery by the delegation of more duties and responsibilities.

It is much better to train and delegate the work to ten people than to do the work of ten people—but it is harder!

40

The ability to delegate responsibility is the fuel that allows common people to attain uncommon results.
~RJS~

Want to be like the very best
companies?
Get lots of feedback.
~RJO~

11

Feedback–The Breakfast Of Service Champs

Isn't it interesting: Companies that are renowned for their service ask for lots of feedback from their customers. Conversely, companies with terrible service never seem to ask. So, are you asking? Ask! Keep asking! Never quit asking! Find as many ways as you can to ask!

There really is only one way to improve something. You have to be able to measure it. If you can't measure it, how will you know if it needs to be improved? The measuring stick for those in business is feedback. Ask a few good open-ended questions, not a yes-or-no question, but questions like these: "What one thing can we do to improve our service?" "What one thing could we do to make our company better for you?"

If you will ask open-ended questions like that, you will get great feedback. You will stay extremely close to your customers and be able to make a tremendous difference.

Here are several ways to get feedback:

- Focus Group - Gather a few of your customers and hear directly from them how they feel about your company.
- Comment Card - Keep a card in a handy place where they can comment when they come into your business.
- Survey - Every two years survey your customer base.
- Ask your customers - Don't miss opportunities to ask how you could do it better.
- An 800 number - Make it easy for people to get a hold of you. By the way, how do you like this book? My number is 800-325-4007.

The Cadillac Of Auto Mistakes

If ever an automaker introduced the wrong car to the wrong market at the wrong time, it was the Ford Motor Company in 1957. Since then, Ford has had to live with the indignity of being responsible for America's most infamous manufacturing disaster—the Edsel! In fact, the Edsel is still used as a term to describe any kind of product or plan disaster. "It's an Edsel" is what you can hear.

The Edsel was advertised and promoted as "the people's choice" after nationwide surveys were conducted to determine exactly what Americans wanted in a new car. Ford executives sifted through reams of market research—and *promptly ignored it!* Instead they built a car by committee. More than 4,000 executive decisions were made on everything from the shape of door handles to the size and shape of bumpers.

Sixteen thousand names were proposed for the Edsel and all were rejected...even those proposed by the poet Marianne Moore, whom Ford had hired to help name the car. It's easy to see why when her choices included "Intelligent Bullet," "Utopian Turtletop," and "Mongoose Civique." The Ford family decided to name the car in memory of Edsel Ford, the only son of Henry. It turned out to be a lousy way to honor someone.

When the car was introduced, people talked about its toilet-seat shaped grille, its widespread winged rear end, and the push- button transmission selector on the hub of the steering wheel. But that's all they did. They didn't buy. And the car was plagued by mechanical gremlins. Ford lost about $3,000 on each car. So after taking a two-year, $350 million bath, Ford relegated the Edsel to the junk yard. According to estimates, it would have been cheaper for Ford to have given away a new Mercury to every Edsel buyer instead of selling them Edsels.

The moral of this sad story: Listen to the feedback! Act upon the feedback! Ask for more feedback!

Every great business is built on customer feedback!
~RJS~

You can be really good
at *what you do*, but you won't
eat well unless people
know *who you are.*
~RJO~

12

If McDonald's Needs To Advertise, How Can You Not?

What would happen if McDonald's quit advertising? We will never know, because it isn't going to happen. They have created worldwide awareness through advertising, and they have no intention of finding out what would happen if they stopped.

So, the question is obvious, if McDonald's needs to advertise can you afford not to? You can be very good at what you do, but you won't eat well if people don't know who you are and what you are all about. You must find a way to tell your story.

Focus on the following when planning your advertising:
  • In what ways are you different and unique?
  • How can you solve people's problems or pain?
  • How can you make it easy to do business with you?
The situation below seems to say it quite well:
A man wakes up after sleeping under an ADVERTISED blanket,
on an ADVERTISED mattress,
and pulls off ADVERTISED pajamas,
bathes in an ADVERTISED shower,
shaves with an ADVERTISED razor,
brushes his teeth with ADVERTISED toothpaste,
washes with ADVERTISED soap,
puts on ADVERTISED clothes,
drinks a cup of ADVERTISED coffee,
drives to work in an ADVERTISED car,
and then refuses to ADVERTISE, believing it doesn't pay.
Later, when his business is poor, he ADVERTISES it for sale.
Why is that? (Author unknown)

The Secret Behind The Golden Arches

Ray Kroc, of McDonald's fame, is one exciting classic example of the person who would never give up on his dream. He didn't hit his stride until he was 52 years old. He began his business career by selling paper cups and playing the piano in gigs to support his family in the early 1920s. He became one of the Tulip Cup Company's top salesmen but gave it all up and struck out on his own in the milk shake business. He sold a machine that could mix a number of milk shakes at a time.

When he heard about the McDonald brothers, who were turning out forty shakes at a time on eight of his multi-mixer machines, he made a special trip out to San Bernardino to investigate. After observing the quality assembly-line production of their burgers, French fries, and milk shakes…he knew this process should not be wasted on only one location.

He asked the McDonald brothers, "Why don't you open other restaurants just like this one?"

They replied: "It would be a lot of trouble, and we don't know who we'd get to open them." Kroc had that person in mind…Ray Kroc.

The most important message in the McDonald's story is that he was able to build McDonald's into a billion-dollar business in only twenty-two years! It took IBM forty-six years to reach one billion in revenues and Xerox sixty-three years!

Ray Kroc's favorite saying was this: "As long as you're green, you're growing; as soon as you're ripe, you start to rot."

The key to McDonald's success can be summed up quite simply: *Do one thing well, until you have mastered it. This will build confidence and a reputation for excellence. Tell it, advertise it, advertise some more and never give up!*

The business that doesn't advertise in order to save money is like the person who unplugs the clock to save time.
~RJS~

Bold plans get the heart
pumping.
Small plans bring about a yawn.
~RJO~

13

Make No Small Plans

I would invite you to take another look at your plans.
- Do they capture people's attention?
- Are they bold?
- Are they aggressive?
- Do they snap people's heads around?
- Do they cause a second look?
- Do people say, "I have never thought of that, what an inspiring plan?"

Bold plans have the ability to stir people's blood. Small plans do little more than bring about a yawn. Could you rework your plans in such a way that they bring people to attention? Perhaps the plan is on a grander scale than they had thought possible. Perhaps the time frame is condensed to the point where it would take a Herculean effort to pull it off. Perhaps the scope of the plan is much more far reaching than anyone anticipated. It is those plans that have a chance of being extremely effective. Many people seem to be drowning in insignificance and would love the chance for the hero to be released within them. Your bold plans can create that very opportunity.

Those same people have not had the chance to commit themselves to something on a grand scale. Perhaps the last thing they did of major significance was in high school. Your bold plan may be the very thing that captivates them. An unknown person from Monticello, Minnesota, decided that something should be done about the effects of tobacco on people. He organized the "National Smoke-Out" day. The impact has been felt worldwide.

If the cause is great, let the plan be equally great!

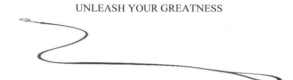

Dream Great Dreams!

Have you experienced a cool refreshing bottle or can of Coke lately? Perhaps even today you've enjoyed it's taste. It's an experience which hundreds of millions of people around the world have enjoyed. In fact, it just might be the single taste treat you and I have in common with more people than any other. How did it come about?

It was because of the huge plans of Robert Woodruff. During his tenure as president of Coca-Cola, from 1923 to 1955, Woodruff boldly declared, "We will see that every man in uniform gets a bottle of Coca-Cola for five cents wherever he is and whatever the costs." And that plan was met with a successful expansion.

When World War II ended, Woodruff made larger plans. He stated that before he died he wanted *every* person in the world to have tasted Coca-Cola at least once!

He's not the only person to have laid out big plans. Take Thomas Watson, Sr., who at age forty joined a company that made products like meat slicers and punch-card machines. The following year he assumed the presidency of this company and nine years later re-named it the International Business Machines Corporation. That is a great name to match a great plan.

Toward the end of his life, Watson was asked this question: "At what point did you envision IBM becoming so big?"

His reply is worth noting: "Right at the beginning!"

When Disney World had the grand opening, Mrs. Walt Disney was asked to speak, since Walt had died before it was completed. She was introduced by the master of ceremonies, "Mrs. Disney, I just wish Walt could have seen this." She stood up and simply said, "He did" and sat down.

Now is the time to ask yourself, *"Is my plan going to make a difference in the world in which I live?"*

Planning puts foundations under our dreams.
~RJS~

Everyone will see the future in time. The leader just happens to be able to see it first.
~RJO~

14

See It Before Others Do

Eventually, everyone sees it. In time, it comes into focus for all. It is just that a leader sees the future long before others do. A leader seems to see things sooner. A leader also seems to see things further down the road. A leader has the ability to look beyond.

Today, we live in a dot-com world. A few saw it long before others did. While some continued to think about better uses for their fax machine, others were inventing the dot-com world.

The future has always belonged to those who have the ability to see it before others do. If every waking hour of the day is spent thinking about the present situation, that is a misuse of time. Start setting aside time each day to look beyond the present situation. See it before others do.

Ask yourself these questions:
- What will people need in the next few years?
- How will the delivery systems change?
- What could I do to make a difference?

Be an eagle, not a chicken. The eagle soars high above the terrain, getting a broad view of everything. The chicken never looks more than a few inches beyond its nose. Find a quiet, inspiring place and take a long range look at the challenges and opportunities ahead.

In the past, if your eyesight was failing, you had two choices—glasses or contacts—and both had their limitations. Today, you have a third option—laser surgery. The solution may seem radical, but the results have been fantastic for many.

It is time for corrective eyesight procedures. Don't be content to just see what is in front of you. See the future before others do.

Filling The Jar

At a "time management" seminar, the speaker addressed a group of high-powered overachievers and said, "Okay, time for a quiz."

He pulled out a one-gallon wide-mouthed mason jar and set it on the table in front of him. Then he produced about a dozen or so fist-sized rocks and carefully placed them, one at a time into the jar. When the jar was filled to the top and no more rocks would fit inside, he asked, "Is this jar full?" Everyone in the class said "Yes."

He replied, "Really?" He reached under the table to pull out a bucket of gravel which he dumped into the jar and shook so that the pieces would work themselves down into the spaces between the big rocks. Then he asked, "Is the jar full?"

The class had caught on. One of the class said, "Probably not." He answered, "Good!" Again, he reached under the table and brought out a small bucket of sand and dumped that sand until all the spaces left between the rocks and gravel were now filled. Once more he asked, "Is this jar full?"

This time, the entire class responded and shouted, "No!" Once more he said, "Good!" Now he grabbed a pitcher of water and poured it in until the jar was filled to the brim. Then he looked at the class and asked, "What is the point of this illustration?"

An eager beaver responded, "No matter how full your schedule is, if you try really hard, you can always fit something more into it." "No," the speaker replied, "that's not the point. The truth is that if you don't put the big rocks in first, you'll never get them in at all."

What do you see as the big rocks of your life, your leadership, your cause, your faith, or your business?

Leadership is about
"seeing" the possibilities
before it's too late.
~RJS~

You may have your master's degree, but until you have mastered the art of affirmation, you still have much to learn.
~RJO~

15

Master The Art Of Affirmation

Why do people stay loyal to their workplace or organization? According to a survey reported in *Industry Week* magazine, the number one factor is job recognition. We all have a great need to be recognized for the work we do.

In order, here are the top five reasons why employees said they were loyal to their company. Number 1 - job recognition. Number 2 - challenging work. Number 3 - increased pay. Number 4 - benefits. Number 5 - dynamic boss. You may or may not be able to do much about numbers 2 - 5, but there is a lot you can do about number 1.

Effective leadership has a lot more to do with influence than it does with position. There is no limit to how you can influence people if you will simply recognize who they are and what they are doing, and let them know about it. Unfortunately, too many people see someone close to them do something well and think to themselves, "she sure did that well. I would never tell her, but she sure did a great job." There is no value there if you think it but don't say it. Mastering the art of affirmation should be like a default setting in your mind. When you see someone doing something well, let them know. That doesn't mean just giving them a plaque at the end of the quarter. There are more short, hand-written letters of expressed thanks hanging in cubicles than there are quarterly plaques.

A few years ago, a woman was named teacher of the year for the country. In an interview, she said that every day she tried to find some way to compliment every one of her students. That may have been the most direct factor in her becoming teacher of the year. That is a lot of compliments. If she teaches thirty students for 180 days in the school year, that is 5,400 compliments. Did you give out 5,400 compliments last year?

Achieving The Peak Performance

In chapter eight, we learned about the inspiring team effort by the workers at the Gruman Aerospace. They were in the process of designing and building the first manned craft to land on the moon. All of us later witnessed the reality on the early morning of July 20, 1969 as we sat glued to our TV sets receiving the transmission from the moon. Gruman had achieved what most had thought to be an impossible mission.

Exactly how had this been achieved? One simple example is shared by the foreman of a department which maintained the plumbing and pipes in the aerospace company's thermodynamics plant. He was able to get high performances from his employees working at low-level jobs. Their jobs were mechanical and repetitive, but his department had the lowest turnover in the company. Why?

Well, now we get down to the nitty-gritty of the concept. This foreman's workers all wear green surgical smocks. He explains, "I got them from my son. He's a cardiovascular surgeon. We are surgeons here, just like my son. He takes care of pipes in the human body. We take care of pipes in the plant." Talk about a positive affirmation! The smart foreman created a dynamic environment which in turn kept these people loyal.

He went on to clarify, "Maintaining the pipes in the plant is as much a part of the big plan of putting a manned vehicle on the moon as anything else that goes on around here. We do our job so that others can do theirs."

Everyone could improve their performance if they received honest affirmation. Develop this leadership skill and use it!

We all live by affirmation
and without it we die—
angrily, slowly, and sadly!
~RJS~

Effective leaders know this:
The more winners,
the greater the win.
~RJO~

16

Be Secure Enough To Let Others Win

A leader not only allows others to rise to greatness, they encourage, push, and promote others to greatness. They understand that if they help enough other people reach their goals they, in turn, will reach their goals and be very successful. A leader knows that any individual glory that they may attain will fall short of the glory that can be attained when a team collectively rises to greatness. There is one trait that must be in place for this to happen; the leader must be secure. How secure? Secure enough to let others win, be noted, receive awards, and get company-wide recognition.

Insecure leaders would never let that happen. Unfortunately, they would find a way to undermine the efforts of others in a hopeless quest to somehow make themselves look better while dragging others down. It may seem like a natural response; unfortunately, it just never works that way. Everyone loses.

So, how can you help others win? It is not just a matter of getting out of their way. It is committing yourself to being proactive in helping them advance their dreams. What encouragement can you provide? What skills do you possess to help them be effective? How can your network be instrumental in helping to make things happen?

The real question seems to be this: Are you self-centered or other-centered? An other-centered focus makes victory all the sweeter. It isn't just a solo flight. It is the exhilaration of bringing many with you on the journey.

There are lots of changes and transitions in your future. Change is not something you do to people. It is something you do with people! There is greatness waiting to be released in people all around you. Help them turn it loose.

Not Your Ordinary Player

Steve Wallace, as a professional football player, has never scored a touchdown in his entire career. He has been one of those unsung heroes who has made a career out of helping others be the well-publicized winners. Oh, yes, Steve has made the All-Star team and played more than once in the Pro Bowl. And during his career, his team, the San Francisco 49ers, compiled an amazing 110 wins and only thirty-three losses. Included in those 110 wins were three Super Bowl Championships!

That's not to say that their success was due entirely to Steve Wallace, but he has been one very vital cog in the Big Red Machine. Mike Solari, 49ers assistant offensive line coach, said, "Steve brings not only physical talents and athletic ability, but also his leadership. He leads his position and our offense as well."

Wallace is a leader. He is big, strong, and he is an extremely hard worker with an immense desire to be the best. And he is intense. Very intense.

"That's the only way to play football!" says this number 74 who wears a huge, double-protective helmet. "You've got to be an intense competitor, giving one hundred percent on every play. You've got to do everything possible to be the best player you can be."

At left tackle, Wallace isn't exactly in position to get the ball often...as his scoring output (zero) would indicate. His role has been to protect the Niners' marquee players like Steve Young, William Floyd, Joe Montana, and Roger Craig. And with more Super Bowl rings in the Niners' locker room than a Jostens' warehouse, Steve has obviously done his job. Wallace stated, "I've got an end zone dance that I've planned for the last 18 years, but I've never scored a touchdown. So I'm still waiting.... But my responsibility is to make others look good, to allow others to score so they can be heroes."

Secure people encourage others to be winners!

One of the most powerful things
in the world is giving somebody
a positive push!
~RJS~

Complex problems sometimes have simple solutions. Learning to 'let it go' can solve many of life's major stressors.
~RJO~

17

Let It Go!

The world of sameness, stability, and tranquility is a distant memory. Our world is all about change, at breakneck speed. Will the company name change, will we be bought out, and will I have a position after the merger? Stress is rampant in the workplace. The heart attack rate among women is way up. Nearly half of all executives will die of a stress-related illness. Is there a solution to the uncertainty of life and the possibility of being blindsided by a raw deal? Yes there is. Three key words make all the difference: Let it go! Some things are simply out of your control, and they will chew you up if you emotionally pitch your tent there. Unfortunately, our reaction to change and stress is often anger. But you must understand this about anger: it only hurts the one carrying it.

So what can be done to let it go? Take a sheet of paper. Divide it into two halves. Label the left half, "Things out of my control." Label the right half, "Things I could change or influence." Make a list of everything that adversely affects you, but is out of your control. Put it on the left-hand side of your sheet. That is the side you need to let go. If you need to, tear off the left side of the page, take the list outside, dig a hole, and have a mock funeral. The right side is where you must spend your energy. Embrace the things that you can do to change or influence the situation. You will find hope flowing through your being one more time.

To "let it go" does not mean giving up. Rather it is using wisdom to choose where to invest your emotional energy. It will insure that your limited resources are focused on those things which have a chance of making a real difference. "Let it go" is your ticket to emotional health and well being.

Hands Off Sally!

While touring Eagle's Rock African Safari Zoo with friends from Russia, Ronald Demuth, from Vermont, found himself in a tough situation. They were at the petting zoo and saw a rhino that was accustomed to being touched by people. Demuth wanted to show his Russian friends the marvelous American invention called "Krazy Glue," so he dramatically put about three ounces of Krazy Glue on the palms of his hands and jokingly placed them on the rump of this petting zoo rhino.

Understand...that in the thirteen years of her life in the petting zoo, "Sally the Rhino" had never before felt any of her viewers leave their hands on her for so long until now! And Sally did not like that sensation. She panicked...running all about the petting zoo with Demuth following closely behind.

Demuth's misfortune was not yet complete. Sally had not been feeling well as of late and her keepers had just given her a laxative and some anti-depressants to relax her bowels. It was great timing when Demuth played his little prank. Sally in her desire to rid herself of the prankster destroyed two fences, three pygmy goats, and one duck. All the while, Demuth was attempting to let her go. During the four hours it took to remove the hands of Demuth from the frightened rhino...the laxatives began to work. Approximately thirty gallons of rhino showers later, Demuth was finally able to let her go, freed from Sally's behind.

Folks...you can't make up stuff like this. It's all true, it did happen. And, by the way, Ronald Demuth's Russian friends were quite impressed.

The moral of this little story is simply: Let it go! Let go of the painful past, let go of your anger, let go of the memories of the raw deal, let it go or become a prisoner to it! Let it go!

We have been given
two incredible things:
ability, and freedom of
choice. Exercise your choice
to let some things go.
~RJS~

What is the best reason to
network? To make yourself
aware of the great, but
hidden, opportunities all
around you.
~RJO~

18

Network Your Way To The Top

Why should you become a great networker? After all, you already know some really good people and you are aware of some really good opportunities. Unfortunately, you just don't know enough. Author Ann Boe laid out an outstanding definition of networking: "Networking is an organized method of making links from the people we know to the people they know, gaining and using an ever-expanding base of contacts." The fact of the matter is that people you already know happen to know very important people for your career and your future. It is a matter of linking with them in ways that allow you to discover who those people are.

Networking is not a self-serving program, moving from person to person like a piranha, trying to discover your next lead or referral. Instead, networking is about finding out what people's dreams are, using your energy to help them realize their dreams, using your references and resourcefulness to help make them more effective. Do that well, and you will both win.

To be a good networker, you must hang out where the people you want to network with hang out. Join a club or group, roll up your sleeves, and become involved in their associations. Get out of your office and start spending time where they are.

The world's first great networker was Joseph. His story was first told in Genesis and most recently in the Broadway Musical *Joseph and the Amazing Technicolor Dreamcoat*. Living in the Mideast thousands of years ago, he faced overwhelming odds. First, his brothers sold him as a slave to Egypt; then he was framed and put in prison in this foreign land. But he networked his way right out of prison. How? He refused to isolate himself, and built relationships with other inmates. One of them was the key to his eventual release.

Nobody Wins Until...

This took place at the "Special Olympics" which were being held in Seattle, Washington. This particular Olympics meet was of national importance...if you won here, you were able to move on to the international competition. The tension in the air could almost be cut with a knife as each was eager to compete. The participants had trained and worked and planned and practiced for these events for months. In fact, they may well have worked harder than any athlete who had ever entered the regular Olympics.

This particular event was a 100-yard-dash heat, a major event. The top three winners would qualify for the final run in this competition.

One very eager young participant, at the sound of the gun, leaped out in front of the others with the best start. However, each foot went in different directions and this well-meaning, well-trained athlete tripped and came tumbling down to the track right in front of the starting blocks!

The other runners, each as eager as he was to compete in this event, stopped running and turned back to help their crying, fallen friend. The crowd was stunned as they observed what was happening down on the track. In this preliminary heat, the crowd came to its feet as his competitors returned to his side, lovingly lifted him up, and walked, arm in arm across the finish line!

They have captured for all of us what true success is all about! In reality, nobody wins until we all win. Networking is defined as making contacts, trading information, and helping others in times of need.

What would happen in your business or personal life if you should take a tumble and nobody was there to help you up again?

Networking allows everybody to be a winner!

A good network is sort
of like a tube of toothpaste—
it comes through in
a tight squeeze.
~RJS~

If you are good at what you do,
and if you can make a difference
in people's lives, refuse to be
unknown.
~RJO~

19

You Cheat Them If You Don't Become Famous

How do you feel about becoming famous? This word conjures up images of outlandish behavior, abuse of power and embarrassing actions. It smacks of "me first!" It seems to go against the philosophy of life that many of us were taught as children.

But, fame in itself is not bad. In fact, it can be used for tremendous good. If Danny Thomas had not become famous, perhaps there would be no St. Jude's Medical Center. If there were no Jerry Lewis, perhaps there would be no Labor Day Tele-a-thon to raise money for muscular dystrophy. Fame, like money, is neutral; it is all in how you use it.

So, how about you? If you don't become famous not only might you lose out on tremendous possibilities in life, but many others may lose out by not getting to know you. Don't cheat the world. Don't cheat yourself. Don't cheat others. Become famous.

Here are some questions to consider:
- Can you improve the quality of someone's life?
- Could someone's life be better because of your help?
- Can you eliminate anyone's pain?
- Can you solve anyone's problems?

If you answered yes, then get going. Find a way to get known. It is possible for anyone to become famous in the same way it is possible for an unknown candidate to put together a great campaign and win an election.

Refuse to be unknown and ignored. Discover your distinctive advantage, your unique ability, and become a recognizable expert in your field. You have my permission to become famous!

Does The Name "Mary Kay" Mean Anything To You?

Mary Kay Ash, CEO for "Mary Kay Cosmetics," understood the importance of seeing the potential in others as well as in herself. She knew this first-hand on both sides of the fence. With two children to support, she began working with "Stanley Home Products" and got off to a miserable start. But as she watched others succeed, she was positive that her own time would come.

Just a short time later, the company scheduled a convention in Dallas. Mary Kay borrowed $12 to pay her way and booked a hotel room. She brought a supply of cheese and crackers to eat for three days. The convention was inspiring, and on the final night, as Mr. Stanley Beverage placed the "Queen of Sales" crown on a brunette, Mary Kay made the decision that started her on the road to success and fame.

As she walked through the receiving line to shake hands with the company president, she looked Stanley in the eyes and said, "Mr. Beverage, you don't know who I am tonight, but this time next year you will, because I am going to be the Queen of Sales!" And she did, next year.

Then she "retired," which lasted about a month. She decided to build her own company on a basis that would utilize the ability she saw in every woman. She saw women capable of earning large sums of money and enjoying the luxuries of life. "Mary Kay Cosmetics" was founded in 1963 and sold $60,000 by year's end. In 1976 they sold over $88,000,000 with more than 40,000 consultants telling the story across the country. And you've also seen those pink Cadillacs! The rest is history.

Mary Kay became famous for her concepts and allowed others to participate in her success.

Nobody has ever traveled
the road to genuine fame
on a free pass.
~RJS~

Never underestimate the power
of being first and the power of
being distinctive.
~RJO~

20

Be Distinctive

Who is Bert Hinkler? Perhaps you are saying, "Can't say that I have heard of him." Who is Charles Lindbergh? Of course you know Lindbergh. He was the first to fly solo across the Atlantic. Bert Hinkler just happened to be number two. He may have flown a more fuel efficient and better mission, but because he was number two, no one knows who he is.

There is something powerful about being first. There is also something powerful about being distinctive. What can you do to distinguish yourself from your competition? Consider the real estate agent who keeps terrific toys in the trunk of his car so that when he talks with mom and dad about buying a house the young children have toys to play with. They can't wait to meet with that realtor again. Or how about the agent that places this slogan on every piece of information that goes out of her office, "Five Star Service." Why does this agent do that? When people think of five stars, they think of the very best. That is how that agent distinguishes herself.

Is there something you do that makes you distinctive? It may be time to leave a tablet by your bed and think about it. When the idea hits you, GO FOR IT! You must find a way to distinguish yourself from the competition.

Consider these questions:
 • What sets me apart?
 • What makes me different from my competitors?

The answer could lie in your unique products, unexpected and exceptional service, or creative and innovative advertising. Find your own niche and use that distinction to become highly valued by your customers.

Wall And Water

In December of 1931, there was nothing distinctive about the drug store in Wall, South Dakota, a little prairie town composed of 326 people.

"Dorothy and I had just bought the only drugstore in a town called Wall on the edge of the South Dakota Badlands. We'd been open a few days and business had been bad," so stated Ted Hustead. Ted had graduated from pharmacy school in 1929 and after two years, decided to find his own store. His father had left a $3,000 legacy with which they made their investment. They settled on Wall because it was a small town and had a Catholic Church. It was a struggle, but they decided to give it five years.

Often Ted minded an empty store, swatting flies, and longingly looked through the window at the traffic driving by on Highway 16A.

Then it happened. One hot Sunday in July of 1936, Dorothy said, "You don't need me here, Ted. I'm going to go put Billy and the baby down for a nap and maybe take one myself."

An hour later Dorothy returned. Ted asked, "Too hot to sleep?" "No, it wasn't the heat that kept me awake," Dorothy said, "It was all the cars going by on Route 16A. The jalopies just about shook the house to pieces." "That's too bad," said Ted.

"No, because you know what, Ted? I think I finally saw how we can get all those travelers to come to our store." She paused, "Well, now what is it that those travelers really want after driving across that hot prairie? They're thirsty. They want water, ice cold water. Why don't we put up signs on the highway telling people to come here for free ice water?" The signs went up, and people came pouring in!

"Free Ice Water," Ted said. "It brought us Husteads a long way and it taught me my greatest lesson...there's absolutely no place on God's earth that's Godforsaken. No matter where you live, you can succeed, because wherever you are *you can reach out to other people with something that they need."*

80

Distinctiveness is usually a do-it-yourself job.
~RJS~

If you are going to spend
the best eight hours of your day
at work, you might as
well enjoy it.
~RJO~

21

Are You Fun To Work With?

Let's be honest, some people aren't really fun to work with. Why is that? Perhaps it is something their parents said when they were little kids. They might have heard, "We're not here to have fun, we're here to work." Unfortunately, they have bought into that and have spent their lives focusing on the seriousness of work.

Don't buy into the myth. Don't be fooled for a moment. America's best companies are having fun in the workplace. They have discovered that workplace fun promotes teamwork, boosts morale and increases productivity.

You don't have to be funny to be fun. Garrison Keeler has said that humor is a presence. The book of Proverbs said it this way, "A merry heart does good like medicine, but a rigid spirit dries up the bones." It is that inflexible, serious spirit that takes the joy out of life.

If you have the ability to draw the best out of others, they will think you quite fun. By listening well to others, by affirming the good work that they do, all will consider you a joy to have around.

Here are a few ideas to get you going. The next time you send out a stressful memo, staple a Kleenex to it. Have everyone bring in their high school yearbook someday. Also, try calling in well. You might say this: "I'm just feeling a bit too good to come in today."

Yes, the best companies in America are having fun. Their workers have humor files. They collect humor resources. They have established humor committees. And they take humor breaks when the heat is on. They have discovered that work and fun do mix really well. You have my permission to lighten up in the workplace.

The Surprise Hitch-Hiker

A family who lived back East had always wanted to take a family trip to the West Coast. It became a family project. The planning was fun. The trip was scheduled for the upcoming summer.

Time drew nearer. The maps were spread out on the table, and carefully, Dad, Mom, and the kids planned the route and where they would stop each night. The trip would be spread out over a six-week period. The time arrived, but there was a problem. The father's work demands prevented him from going. Mom insisted that she was capable of driving and that she and the kids would go ahead and take the trip. To cancel would be a huge disappointment.

A couple of weeks later, the father managed to complete his extra responsibilities. He decided to surprise the family so he booked a flight to a West Coast city without calling them. Then he took a taxi out into the country on a highway that, according to their travel plans, the family should be driving on later that day.

The taxi driver dropped him off on the side of the road. Dad waited patiently there until he saw the family car coming…then he stuck out his thumb to hitch a ride.

As mom and the kids drove past, they did a double-take! One of the kids shouted, "Hey! Wasn't that Dad?!" Mom screeched to a stop, backed up to the hitch-hiker, and the family had a joyful roadside reunion!

A newspaper reporter picked up on the story and managed to find them at a local motel for an interview. The reporter asked the father *why* he would do such a crazy thing. This dad responded: "After I die, I want my kids to be able to say, 'Dad sure was fun!'"

Wouldn't it be great to be remembered as a fun person to work or live with?

84

You don't have to teach people
to have fun on the job…
you only need to give them
permission.
~RJS~

There is a hero locked up
inside of all those around you.
You hold the key.
~RJO~

22

You Can Build Heroes

Look around, what do you see? Perhaps you see men whose ties are too short, women with runs in their nylons, balding men using a hairstyle designed to fool others that just isn't working. Is that what you see? Is that all you see? If so, you are missing a lot. There is a hero within every person we encounter; it is simply a matter of finding a way to turn that loose.

Lack of creativity is usually not the issue. Freeing people up to use their creativity is paramount. When creativity is tapped, there is an opportunity for the hero within to emerge. What can you do to place people in a position to become heroes? How can you best tap their creativity? How can you turn loose the best possibilities within them?

Your interest, your affirmation, your thoughtfulness can bring it out of each of them. You can create heroes. You create a hero every time you put other people in a situation where they can win. You create heroes by giving others the opportunity to solve a problem creatively.

It all starts with your perception of others. If you focus on their limitations and shortcomings, you will have ample evidence that your analysis was correct. If you see them as unique creations, you will discover untapped possibilities. There is a hero within each person just waiting to come out.

Consider this as a new way to view your job description; you are in the business of building heroes. You have the ability to help others see what they have not seen and discover what they never knew was within them.

You Are A Lousy Football Player

During a practice session for the Green Bay Packers, things were not going well for Vince Lombardi's team. Lombardi singled out one huge guard for his failure to "put out." It was a hot muggy day when the coach called his guard aside and leveled his awesome verbal guns on him as only Lombardi could: "Son, you are a lousy football player! You're not blocking! You're not putting out. As a matter of fact, it's all over for you today, go take a shower!"

The big guard dropped his head and walked to the dressing room. Forty-five minutes later when Lombardi walked in, he saw the big guard sitting in front of his locker still in uniform. His head was bowed and he was sobbing quietly.

Lombardi did something that was typical of him. He walked over to the player, sat next to him, and put an arm around his shoulder. "Son," he said, "I told you the truth. You are a lousy football player. You're not blocking, you're not tackling, and you're not putting out. HOWEVER, in all fairness to you, I should have finished the story. Inside of you, son, there is a great football player and I'm going to stick by your side until the great football player inside of you has a chance to come out and assert himself!"

With those words ringing in his ears, Jerry Kramer straightened up, held his head high, and felt better. As a matter of fact, he felt so much better that he went on to become one of the all-time greats in football and was voted the best "all-time" guard in the first fifty years of professional football.

That was Lombardi! He saw things in people that they seldom saw in themselves. He had the ability to inspire his people to use the talent they had. His players gave him three consecutive World Championships!

You're surrounded by heroes and achievers...just affirm them!

People become heroes
because they were courageous
for thirty seconds longer
than the average person.
~RJS~

There will always be a place in this world for the person who solves problems instead of shelving them.
~RJO~

23

Have A Fixation
With Finding Solutions

This is the language of problem-oriented people. They walk into the supervisor's office and say the following: "This is a real mess, yep, this is the big one. I don't know how you are going to sort this one out, but good luck. That's why we pay you the big bucks." For problem-oriented people, dumping problems on others is a way of life.

To really impact people you must have a fixation with finding solutions. All around are problems to be solved. To become invaluable, simply seek out those problems and use your creative energy to solve them. You can find them at home, at work, in your community, your neighborhood, your church, your organization. There is no shortage of problems. Unfortunately, there seems to be a shortage of solution-oriented people.

The way the world works is really quite simple: if you solve little problems, you will make a little money. However, if you solve big problems, you have the opportunity to make big money. And to make a true impact, seek out all the biggest problems you can find and use all your resourcefulness to solve those problems.

Problems are really opportunities in work clothes. They do come disguised, of course, but they are there right in front of you—providing you an opportunity to become invaluable. Ask yourself these questions:

- What could I do to make a difference?
- What could I do to solve the problem?
- What steps could I take to move the problem off center?
- Who will be instrumental in helping to solve this problem?

Answer these questions, and your life will soon get very exciting. In a world where many want someone else to solve it or fix it, you will become a true person of impact.

If You Want It Done Right

This report concerns some Benedictine monks in Virginia who support their order with a fruitcake business—baking and selling them, especially for the Christmas season. This small business began doing so well that the monks contacted a computer consultant to set up their business on computers.

While training the monks to use his computers, the consultant observed something. It was an opportunity for some additional business for them. He established the monks as data entry clerks for hospitals and major corporations...sending their data to the companies via e-mail.

This concept worked so well with these Benedictine monks, under the direction of this consultant, that word soon spread and now there are numerous orders of monks and nuns who have joined the data entry business.

This is not the end of this story. The consultant who originated this lucrative business enterprise and the companies who contracted for the monks' services made a very pleasant unexpected side benefit discovery. This benefit has been a regular boon to the hospitals, clinics, and other businesses that use the services of these religious orders. Well, what is it? The work is tedious and secular, but...the benefit is that these monks and nuns have no outside or worldly distractions in their lives so their entry work is virtually error and mistake free!

As you learn to find solutions, everyone comes out ahead!

Problems should not merely
be faced…they should
be attacked!
~RJS~

Business cards are the
currency of networkers.
Don't leave home without them.
~RJO~

24

Use A Business Card Wisely

So, what do you do with that business card you just picked up? Perhaps you put it in your shirt pocket, bring it home at the end of the day and set it on the top of your dresser. After sometime, your spouse asks you to clean off the top of your dresser. You get a rubber band, group several cards together and slide them into your sock drawer. Is that how you treat a business card? Unfortunately, many do. Don't you ever, *ever*, **ever** treat a business card that way. That business card not only represents one very important person, it also represents the hundreds of people that that person knows.

You see, a business card is really the currency of networkers. It is the finest way to give somebody succinct, but important, information so that they can get a hold of you and you can get a hold of them.

Every time you get a business card, there are three things you should do. Number one: place the date on the front of it. That way you will never forget when it was you met that person. Number two: write a brief message on the back concerning the things you talked about. That way you will never forget what it was you discussed. Number three: put the card in a notebook so that you can visually see it and stay connected. Obviously, you can use your computer to organize your network, but you may find it very helpful to be visually stimulated by a folder of business cards.

Every business card represents unlimited opportunities. If you have the business cards of ten well-connected people, you potentially have the ability to connect with a thousand resourceful people. Collect them frequently, give them away often, and remember, don't put them in your sock drawer!

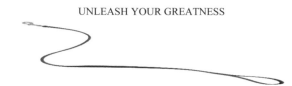

The First Use
Of A Business Card?

"Please give my friend Mr. Perkins a good position in your Department, and oblige yours truly, - A. Lincoln." This message was written on a small card and handed to the Secretary of the Treasury. The signature was apparently that of the president, so the bearer was installed into a clerkship at $1,600 a year. Three months passed when Eli Perkins appeared at the secretary's desk with another card: "Please promote my friend, the bearer, and oblige yours truly, - A. Lincoln."

He was raised to $2,000 a year for three months when a similar card procured another raise of $400. The other clerks were astonished at the rapid promotion of the most strictly ornamental loafer in the department.

The secretary, while riding with the president, remarked that he had attended to his wishes regarding Mr. Perkins. The president replied that he knew no such a person and an investigation was launched.

Mr. Perkins appeared before the president and confessed to Mr. Lincoln that he had been animated by a desire to serve the nation and had used his name on the business cards afore mentioned…but also pleaded that he had done the president no wrong.

"Now, Mr. President," he said winningly, taking a card from his pocket, "do me the favor to glance at this." This card read: "Mr. Secretary, please have Mr. Perkins furnished with champagne cocktails every two hours while on duty and charge the same to the Stationery Fund. Yours truly, - A. Lincoln."

The President read the card, his lips twitched nervously for a moment or two and something like a cough-suppressed chuckle was heard as he tried unsuccessfully to frown. At last he said, "You may go, Mr. Perkins."

Eli made for the door, with his hand on the knob, turned, smiled and murmured, "Mr. President, my position, shall I…?" "You may keep it for the present, sir," Lincoln replied. Ah, yes… *the value of the business card should not be underestimated!*

A business card is to business
what fertilizer is to farming.
~RJS~

If George Washington and Jesus had difficult people in their lives, there is a good chance you will have a few in your life as well.

~RJO~

25

Limit The Difficult People In Your Life

Wouldn't it be wonderful if you had no difficult people in your life? It seems to me that if George Washington had Benedict Arnold and Jesus had Judas, then who are you and I to think that we can waltz through life without any difficult people? I am convinced that everyone deserves at least one difficult person in his or her life.

Some people just seem to have a lot more difficult people in their lives than others. Is it possible to limit the difficult people in your life? I think so. You can start by assuming that everyone likes you. Use all of your energy in a positive way to treat them like best friends. You will be able to convert many difficult people into friendly allies. Also, to eliminate difficult people in your life, you must look for the good in others. Is that your focus or do you spend much of your energy finding faults, problems, and flaws? Whatever you are looking for, you will be sure to find it.

Another key is to make sure you don't let other people's problems become your own. You lose perspective and the ability to bring about a solution if you get mired down with the problems of others. Have empathy, but stay focused on finding the solution.

Lastly, the worst thing you can do if you have a difficult person in your life, is to go on avoiding the source of difficulty. You must deal directly with this person concerning his or her difficult behavior. Does he approach life like a Sherman Tank, running over everyone in his path? You must confront him or he will keep on running over people, feeling others are inferior. Does she throw a bucket of cold water on every idea you throw out there? Don't let her get away with it. Force her to come up with another idea. No one has the right to shoot down an idea and simply walk away. Unfortunately, you will always have difficult people in your life. The good news is that you can limit the number of difficult people in your world.

It's A Classic

In his classic, *Les Miserables,* Victor Hugo tells the story of Jean Valjean, whose only crime in life was stealing a single loaf of bread in order to feed his sister's starving children. Just one loaf. After serving nineteen years in prison, Valjean was released. He searched for work, but because of his prison record, was unable to find any. Valjean finally made his way to the home of an elderly bishop where he was given supper and a bed for the night.

During supper, Valjean ate off beautiful silver plates. He marveled at the fact that he, a recent prisoner, was eating from such elegant ware. As he lay in bed, he thought of their value. He got out of bed earlier than the rest of the household and, yielding to the temptation, stole the silver plates, slipping out of the house under cover of darkness. But he was soon caught by the police and returned to the bishop's home.

"This man stole your plates," said the policeman. The kind bishop told the officer, "Why, I gave them to him. And Jean, you forgot to take the candle sticks."

Jean Valjean was so overwhelmed at the bishop's display of kindness that he became a Christian. This simple act of kindness brought about a complete change in his life. You need to read the story to discover how completely this life was changed.

It's absolutely amazing what can happen in human relationships as a result of an honest act of kindness! Plagued by difficult people in your life? *Perhaps taking the high road and exercising a bit of kindness will make the difference.*

> *Heretic, rebel, a thing to flout,*
> *But love and I had the wit to win,*
> *We drew a circle and took him in.*

Don't allow the difficult
people of your life
to use you
for a dumping station.
~RJS~

Your future is limited only by the
size of your thoughts.
~RJO~

26

Think Big, It Pays Better

So, are the rich really working that much harder than you are? Probably not. Are they putting in a lot more hours than you are? I doubt it. So, why does it seem to be working so much better for them? Your effectiveness has everything to do with the way you think. If you begin to think bigger, you will discover that it pays better. Are you a community-wide thinker? Then begin to expand and become a city-wide thinker. Or, are you a city-wide thinker? Stretch out; think on a state-wide level. Let's say you are already there; think nationally. If you happen to be a national thinker, think worldwide!

Take the project; magnify it, multiply it, expand it. You must allow the energy of the possibilities help you overcome the sapping effects of obstacles and naysayers. Hey, someone dared to dream that every home would have a personal computer. That was a big thought! It's soon to become a reality. You probably can't work any harder, but you can think bigger.

One of the keys to thinking bigger is to "run with the runners." Find people who think the way you would like to think and spend time with them. Perhaps they would allow you to shadow them for a day. Seeing how they do things, how they set up their business, may be just the push you need to break through your self- imposed limitations.

To think big, you will find yourself swimming upstream like a salmon. Most people are content just to float along with the current. It is easier, and there is very little opposition. Your encouragement will not come from the masses but from a select few who have overcome the numbing effects of small thinking.

Participant Or Spectator?

Well-known coach Lou Holtz proclaimed: "I'm a firm believer in goals. Take a good look at me. You'll notice I stand five feet ten, weigh 152 pounds, wear glasses, speak with a lisp, and have a physique that appears like I've been afflicted with beriberi or scurvy most of my life. The only reasons why I can stand up as head football coach at the University of Notre Dame are that I have a great wife and I am very goal-oriented."

In 1966 Lou Holtz was unemployed. He then listed on a piece of paper 107 lifetime goals. Among them was to be chosen as head coach of the Notre Dame football team. He also listed a goal to have dinner at the White House, make an appearance on the "Tonight Show," jump out of a plane, and many other aspirations. "Don't be a spectator," Holtz exhorts, "don't let life pass you by."

Chuck Givens' name isn't exactly a household word; but he would whole-heartedly agree with Coach Holtz. As a kid, Chuck wrote down 181 goals he wanted to achieve in his lifetime. First on his list was to write a song that would hit the top of the country music charts...which he did at the age of 22. His hit song "Hang On Sloopy" earned him enough money that he could start his own recording studio. A few weeks later it burned to the ground, yet Givens believed if he could do it once, he could do it again. To date, Givens has achieved 160 of his 181 goals and he keeps going on!

Helmut Schmidt wrote, "It must be born in mind that the tragedy of life doesn't lie in not reaching your goal. The tragedy lies in having no goal to reach. It isn't a calamity to die with dreams unfulfilled, but it is a calamity not to dream. It is not a disgrace not to reach the stars, but it is a disgrace to have no stars to reach for. Not failure, but low aim is sin."

So now, it's question time: How many goals have you set? And what price are you willing to pay to make them come true?

Think big! Think out of the box! Think creatively! Go for it!

Whatever the mind can
conceive and believe
it can also achieve.
~RJS~

There is no better friend to a
leader than the question,
What if?
~RJO~

27

What If? Ask It Often

Is there anything more stimulating than a well-asked question? Has there ever been a finer question than, *What if?* Some people seem to approach life by focusing in on what is. They are implementers. They can take what is at hand, work with it and improve it by making slight adjustments. Others have the ability not to be limited by what they see. They look beyond; they ask the question, *What if?* They are the innovators, never content with what is, but always looking at the possibilities that lie beyond.

The *What if?* question speaks of hope. It speaks of trust in the future, of betterment, of improvement. No matter how good something is presently, it could be improved, it could be expanded, and it could be made better. *What if?* is the question that leads to exploration, to discovery. It is a question that causes your brain to be stimulated, your pulse rate to pick up, and your creative energy to flow. Ask it often!

So how do you get started? Here are some questions you should ask:

- What are you not content with?
- What areas in your life/business represent unrealized potential?
- What are your unrealized dreams?

After you answer those questions, ask the *what if* question and plan to explore lots of creative options. Brainstorm, make lengthy lists, and take the lid off the possibilities. Come up with outrageous plans, plans that make you laugh because they are so outside the normal realm of your thought processes. Most of those options will not be the ultimate answer, but somewhere in that list may be the captivating idea that energizes everyone and sets you on a discovery course that brings about a remarkable new solution.

The People Business

Late in his career, Stanley Arnold, called the "million-dollar-idea-man," was working at Young and Rubicam, where he was asked to come up with a marketing campaign for Remington Rand. The company was among the most conservative in America, and its chairman, appropriately enough, was General Douglas MacArthur. Intimidated at first by a company that was so much a part of America, Arnold also found in that phrase the first inspiration for a campaign. After two weeks of thinking about what it meant, he paid a personal visit to the New York offices of Merrill-Lynch and placed with them the ultimate odd-lot order: "I want to purchase," he told the broker, "one share of every single stock listed on the New York Stock Exchange."

The broker was astonished: "Mr. Arnold, we believe in diversification, but this is incredible."

"I'm glad to hear it," said Arnold, who had worked hard to elicit just such a response.

After a vice president attempted to talk him out of it, the order was placed. It came to more than $42,000 for one share in each of 1,098 companies. Arnold then took this diversified portfolio into a meeting of Remington Rand's board of directors, where he argued passionately for a sweepstakes campaign with the top prize called "A Share in America." The conservative old gentlemen shifted around and discussed the idea.

"But Mr. Arnold, we are not in the securities business," said one. "We are in the shaver business," added another. "I agree that you are not in the securities business, but I think you also ought to realize that you are not in the shaver business. You are in the people business!" so said the idea man. "One more thing to consider gentlemen: What if...?" The company bought the idea! *What if!*

The neatness of a theory
may be no match for the
messiness of reality.
~RJS~

Everyone is anxious
to hear about the cure
if it will stop their pain.
~RJO~

28

Find The Pain

Question: Who has pain? Answer: Everyone. Question: What are they looking for? Answer: A cure. Question: How do you find your niche in life? Answer: Identify the pain and suggest the cure.

If you can find the pain, and if you can help the cure, there will always be a place for you in this world. Your approach should be to discover the pain. Ask questions like these: What isn't working? What is causing you sleepless nights? What is your dream for your organization? What do you wish could be improved? Discover the answer to those questions and you are very close to becoming a person of great impact. It is then simply a matter of setting out to discover the cure.

This is, in effect, what sales is all about—when it is conducted on the highest level. It is not about pushing products on people; it is all about being a professional problem solver and stopping the pain. It is caring enough to know what isn't working for someone and helping them find the cure.

"Seek first to understand, then to be understood" is the advice Steven Covey gave us in the book *Seven Habits of Highly Effective People*. Your effectiveness with others goes way up when you focus first on understanding them. Take a genuine interest in them and find out what you can do to help them remove the pain in their lives.

Another way to look at it is this: Keep in focus the method doctors always follow. They diagnose, and then they prescribe. They never deviate from that formula. It is the diagnosis that allows them to eliminate all the inappropriate cures. A correct diagnosis allows them laser-like accuracy in solving the problem.

Use the same formula. Diagnose the problem, find the pain, and apply the cure.

Healing The Pain

Dr. Richard Selzer, formerly a surgeon/instructor at the University of Dallas Medical School has been called a "craftsman with pen and scalpel." He is now retired and devoting more of his time to writing. He spoke once of searching "for meaning in the ritual of surgery, which is at once murderous, painful, healing, and full of love."

In his book, *"Letters to a Young Doctor,"* Dr. Selzer writes about accompanying a surgeon, during his residency, to Honduras on a medical mission of mercy. One of the young doctor's patients, a young girl, came to them with a cleft lip and palate, a deformity of the mouth and lip so grotesque she would not remove the cloth which she always held over her mouth to shield her imperfection.

Tragically, during the surgical procedure, the young girl died—a totally unforeseen reaction to the anesthetic. The operation was halted midway, only half completed.

At the funeral, the girl's mother greeted Dr. Selzer with profuse thanks, for her daughter had gone to heaven with the resurrected beauty for which she had long prayed. The young doctor, Selzer realized, had slipped into the hospital morgue at night and completed his surgery, repairing the deformity. What an act of vanity and denial, Selzer had thought at first. But in the retelling of this story, more than a decade later, Selzer now sees the doctor differently. "I would like to have told him what I know now, that his unrealistic act was one of goodness, an act to heal the pain, one of those persevering acts done, perhaps, to ward off madness."

Without acts of compassion, there can be no meaningful human relationships. Without help, our society breaks down. Without healing, business life cannot be nurtured. *Therefore...learn to find the need and fill it, find the pain and do what you can to cure it!*

Everybody has a pain,
is a pain,
or has to live with a pain.
It's our opportunity to
find a cure for it.
~RJS~

Who do people with problems gravitate to? Anyone who can solve their problems.
~RJO~

29

Solve The Unsolved Problems

Gandhi, Lincoln, Mandella, King; what do they all have in common? They identified the greatest problems of their day and then used their energy to solve them.

Steven Covey has said that the world of unsolved problems represents your greatest opportunity in the business world today. Your office has unsolved problems, your church has unsolved problems, and your community has unsolved problems. Every organization does. To be a person of impact, you must focus on the unsolved problems of your day.

It starts with a desire to make a difference. It grows as your discontent with the situation intensifies. It reaches critical mass when you decide that the situation cannot go on any longer. Something must be done, and you are not content to sit back and wait for someone else to step up to bat.

What is it that keeps us from taking action and attacking the problem? Perhaps it is the unknown. We know that something should be done, we just don't know how.

Here is an extremely critical point. You will figure out the "what" long before you figure out the "how." In other words, the solution will not come to you right away. It will develop as you give energy to solving the problem. You will know that something needs to be done long before you know exactly how it should be done.

Make a commitment to solving the problem. Immerse yourself in the situation. As you do, your creative juices will flow, you will find others rising up around you to lend their energy, and the "how" will become known to you after you commit to solving the problem.

Landings Need Improvement

The New Guinean tribesmen's introduction to the white man's "Balus" or "bird" was sometimes traumatic, sometimes humorous.

In the 1950s, pilot Peter Manser, who was flying a Taylorcraft Auster J-5, was taking a young man of the Dreikikir tribe back home from a farm where he had been working. He was the only passenger along with Peter. The passenger, who had never flown in a plane, sat nervously alongside the pilot, clutching his ax and a red wood box of trade goods.

Quite suddenly the engine stopped. Manser, realizing they were about to crash, reached past his petrified passenger and opened the door. In a pidgin type of dialect, he yelled, "As we hit the treetops, jump out of the plane quickly!"

Moments later they stalled out onto the dense jungle canopy. The young man bailed out still holding his precious possessions. The thick vegetation broke his fall and he came to a stop on the ground—a bit bruised but not seriously injured—about 100 yards from the crashed Auster and the now unconscious pilot.

He was more than a bit angered by the whole business and gathered his possessions and stomped off toward his village. Manser recovered from the crash and was present some time later when his passenger was questioned about the crash by government investigators.

They had great difficulty keeping straight faces when the young man, in pidgin, told them that he would be happy to fly again in the white fellow's "big Balus" but wished they could somehow provide a better way of getting off the big bird.

Finding the solutions and solving the problems is your most exciting opportunity in today's business world!

One of the most noble
things in this world
is to assist another
human being in solving the
unsolvable.

~RJS~

Give them a reason to ignore you and they will. Give them a reason not to and they won't.
~RJO~

30

No Action, No News

Do people know who you are? Are they talking about you? Is there an awareness of who you are? There is an old axiom in journalism that states, "No action, no news." You must give them a reason to talk about you. You have to create some action. Do nothing and you will be ignored. Do something and you will create a stir. As Tom Peters would say, it takes "a bias for action."

What action can you take to get them talking? What will cause people to take notice? Come up with a bold plan or tackle a challenging problem, and you will not be ignored.

And how do you get the word out? As Jeffrey Davidson would say, you have to "blow your own horn." Don't be shy about telling your story. There are lots of ways to let people know.

Write a press release and submit to the newspapers in the area where you are focusing. Answer the "who, what, why, where, when, and how" questions and submit your release.

Be a guest on local radio talk shows and tell the story of what you are doing. Come up with several interesting questions for your host to ask you.

Tell your story at a local Chamber of Commerce or Rotary meeting. The Chamber usually has a monthly guest speaker and the Rotary is looking for a presenter every week. There are also possibilities for getting on your local cable programs.

The greatest energy a spaceship exerts is overcoming the pull of gravity in escaping the earth's atmosphere. Your greatest challenge will be overcoming inertia. An object at rest tends to remain at rest. Make a commitment to developing a bias for action. People will be talking.

How Silly Putty Bounced Back

A funny thing happened as the government searched for a rubber substitute during World War II. At General Electric's New Haven laboratory, a chemical engineer, James Wright, was assigned the task. He mixed silicone oil and boric acid in a test tube. Presto! They combined into a pink gooey polymer. He was excited and threw it down on the counter!

Pow! To his great delight and surprise, it bounced back! With high hopes, GE sent gobs of the substance to scientists around the world challenging them to find some uses for it. They couldn't come up with any.

So "bouncing putty," as GE dubbed it, languished. But some fun-loving scientists mixed up small batches for parties. After one such affair in Connecticut in 1949, a glop of the stuff was given to Peter Hodgson, Sr., a high school dropout, advertising consultant, and bon vivant. As he fingered and massaged it, the phrase "silly putty" popped into his head. Although already some $12,000 in debt, he borrowed $147 more and bought twenty-one pounds of the putty from GE at $7 a pound. He packed it into little plastic eggs and began selling it as an adult toy at an incredible markup of $2 per half ounce.

Hodgson was doing pretty well, selling as many as three hundred eggs a day to a few retail outlets, when a reporter from the *New Yorker* featured the putty in a small story. Within just a few short days, he received orders for 230,000 eggs! Silly Putty, "the toy with one moving part," was now on its way to becoming a national mania, thanks to the action created with media help! And as they say…the rest is history.

Give them a good, positive reason to talk about you!

The best time to do something worthwhile and news-worthy is between yesterday and tomorrow.
~RJS~

The day of the lone ranger
approach to business
is long over.
~RJO~

31

Don't Be A Lone Ranger

While we admire the rugged individualism of the Lone Ranger, it is the person who knows how to create a team that makes great strides forward. Ask yourself this question: Who could win by being involved with me and how could I win by being involved with them? There are many people who would profit a great deal by linking themselves with you and your venture. Don't go it alone—team up. Find ways for everyone to win. Many times, you will be able to share advertising costs, hot leads and referrals. And working together creates a synergy that is impossible by yourself.

The best Real Estate agents across the country are doing it. So are the best insurance agents, financial planners, etc. Individualism is lonely, costly, and far less effective. Create a dynamic team around you.

And what is needed to create this kind of team? A pied piper. That's right. It calls for someone who will take the initiative to call key people together and lay out a vision of increased effectiveness through a team approach.

Someone has said there are only two kinds of people in the world: those who have gone through transition and those who will go through transition. At a time of career transition, the natural tendency is to become depressed and move into an isolation mode. Avoid this at all costs. It is the kiss of death. If ever you need to expand your network, if ever you need to surround yourself with a team of dynamic people, it is in a time of transition! As Anne Boe said, "Networking is the safety net beneath your career tightrope."

Leave your "go it alone" approach on the golf course. Multiply the possibilities of your life by creating a dynamic team around you.

The Safety Bulletin

TO THE WORKERS' COMPENSATION COURT: I am writing in response to your letter regarding my worker compensation injury report. In block #3 of the accident form, I put "attempting to do the job alone" as the cause of my accident. You said in your letter that I should explain more fully.

I am a bricklayer. On the day of the accident, I was working alone on the roof of a new six-story building. When I completed my work, I discovered I had about 600 pounds of brick left over. Rather than carry the bricks down by hand I decided to lower them in a barrel by using a pulley, which was attached to the side of the building at the sixth floor.

Securing the rope at ground level, I went up to the roof, swung the barrel out and loaded the brick into it. Then I went back to the ground and untied the rope, holding it tightly to insure a slow descent of the 600 pounds of brick. You will note in block #11 that I weigh 155 lbs.

Due to my surprise at being jerked off the ground, I lost my presence of mind and forgot to let go of the rope. I proceeded at a rapid rate up the side of the building. In the vicinity of the third floor, I met the barrel coming down. This explains the fractured skull and broken collarbone.

Slowed slightly, I continued my ascent, not stopping until my fingers were squashed deep into the pulley. The barrel of brick hit the ground and the bottom fell out. Devoid of the brick, the barrel weighed about fifty pounds. Refer to block #11. I then began a rapid descent. In the vicinity of the third floor, I met the barrel coming up. This accounts for the two fractured ankles and lacerations of my legs. This encounter slowed me enough to lessen my injuries when I fell onto the pile of bricks and only three vertebrae were cracked. However, as I lay there on the brick, in pain, unable to stand, and watching the empty barrel six stories above me, I once again lost my presence of mind...and let go of the rope. *No more attempting to do it all alone.*

If you don't think teamwork
is necessary, watch what happens
to a car when one wheel falls off.
~RJS~

The best way to leave a legacy
is to reproduce yourself.
~RJO~

32

Reproduce Yourself

There is no finer legacy than to reproduce yourself. So, whom have you trained, or mentored, or inspired? You can multiply your effectiveness by investing wisely in someone else.

There is a simple formula to follow in your quest to reproduce your effectiveness:

- You do it. It simply means that whatever it is you want others to do, it is imperative that you do it first in your own life. You really can't teach others to do things that you don't do yourself.
- You do it - they watch. There are a lot of ways to train and inspire someone. You can send them to a conference or have them watch a video; but there is no finer way to train someone than to allow them to watch you in action.
- They do it - you watch. Step three is every bit as vital as step two. Allow them to do it and be close at hand to observe how they do it. If they make an error, you can correct it. If they achieve, you can affirm them. If they are flustered, you can solve the problem. Don't miss the importance of this step!
- They do it - others watch. You have now multiplied the effectiveness of your life. What you began in a one-on-one process is now being duplicated many times over.

You have a choice in life. Do what you do and when you are done enjoy the fruits of your labor. Or, do what you do and allow others to be close enough to watch, learn, and capture your vision. Now your efforts do not cease, but by reproducing your life, you continue to impact the world. Leave a legacy.

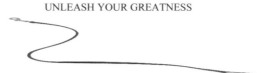

Empowering Others To Produce

Alvin Burger was shouted down and driven off the speaker's platform at a meeting of the "Florida Pest Control Association" in 1960 when he made a suggestion. Exterminators, as a general rule, paid employees poorly and trained them erratically, if at all. "Standards" were set by the customer. In the view of Burger, all of the above added up to sloppy and poor service.

"I think it is unethical to make money for poor quality performance," he said. "It doesn't have to be this way," he continued. "We can improve our service by paying more attention, and more money, to the people we hire." His colleagues and competitors hooted in derision. Burger listened, and then headed for the door. Just before leaving, he looked back and announced: "I quit!"

Those were far from his last words on the subject. In fact, he has made his personal standards the standards for an entire industry. He started his own company, named Bugs Burger Bug Killers, Inc., which is today known as the Mercedes of the extermination business.

To a person, his employees are dedicated to absolute quality! And their key is effective teamwork among themselves and their customers.

Another key is that Burger has learned how to mentor others in order to bring out the best of their own capabilities. For every fifty applicants, Burger will hire one. He puts that new employee through a rigorous five-month training/mentoring program. People who know compare it to boot camp in the army, only "three times as long and twice as difficult." Nobody in his organization has any difficulty in understanding Al Burger's definition of acceptable performance.

A district manager, who contracts for their services, says: "This is the only company I ever saw where the owner and the people on the job all think the same way."

Mentoring is a key to producing superior results!

128

The mediocre mentor tells,
the good mentor explains,
the superior mentor
demonstrates,
the great mentor inspires,
the best mentor reproduces
another mentor.
~RJS~

The best way to begin thinking like a top producer is to spend time with a top producer.
~RJO~

33

Develop A Top Producer's Mindset

How does a top producer think? What is the thought process of a person of impact? One phrase seems to best capture the essence of the mindset of a top producer: Have a bias for action. A top producer is not content to think about it, brainstorm, reflect upon it or kick the idea around. The top producer has an unswerving commitment to action. Mental gymnastics may be necessary but will not get the job done. It is a commitment to doing—a bias for action—that makes great things possible. Top producers have the ability to roll up their sleeves, get to work and make it happen.

How do you want to be known? As someone who has the ability to dream dreams or as someone who makes things happen? Perhaps you have been philosophizing long enough. It is time to get to work. Develop a bias for action.

It would be wise to figure out who are the very best at doing what you desire to do. They have developed a top producer's mindset. They have worked out a plan that has helped them reach peak production. And they are worth emulating.

They may be across the city or they may be across the country. Either way, it would be one of the finest investments you could ever make to go see them and learn what you can. Why reinvent the wheel?

Discover their motivation, their approach, and how they stay on track. If "a picture is worth a thousand words," a look at the setup of a top producer would surely be worth thousands of dollars.

It is usually not talent that separates people at the top. There is no shortage of talented failures. The key is perseverance and tenacity. Develop the mindset of a top producer.

American Dreams

As far back in his life as he can remember, Tom Monaghan, the founder of Domino's Pizza, has been dreaming huge dreams. And looking at his background would not lead one to believe that an achiever would ever come from such a life. He was orphaned quite early in life from a poverty stricken family in upper rural Michigan.

The dreams became more refined and focused as Tom entered his teens. His one big dream was to be the owner of the Detroit Tigers baseball team one day.

He had other dreams. Not having a lot of patience with the slow pace of college, he dropped out and started a tiny pizza store in 1960. From that small beginning he, today, runs the world's largest pizza delivery company. From that single store, he now owns a franchise of more than 4,100 stores with sales topping out at the $4 billion mark. He is still growing and employs more than 150,000 people. And, of course, he is the owner of the Detroit Tigers, having paid $53 million for the baseball team in 1983.

But that's not the real point of this story. "Dreaming is the greatest preparation for wealth," Tom Monaghan told *The Los Angeles Times* in an interview.

Tom went on to say, "When the opportunities came, I think I was ready to act on them. A lot of people around me would see me doing things that made no sense to them at all…but I had a big jump on them. I was thinking about these things years ago." And he took the required actions to make all a reality!

It's thinking, dreaming, planning…and then comes the action!

Actions are contagious,
but don't wait
to catch them from others.
Be a carrier!
~RJS~

Some things can be left
at home.
Enthusiasm is not one of them.
~RJO~

34

Enthusiasm—Don't Leave Home Without It!

So, you say you're whipped. You've just had a Murphy's Law day; in fact, the worst day you can remember. If it could go bad, it did go bad. The result: you are absolutely drained at the end of the day, no strength left. The night calls for lying on the couch with the remote in one hand, a bag of chips and an ice-cold soda close by. Your spouse meets you at the door and explains you are needed for a project that will take about three hours of your evening. You protest and explain that you have never had a worse day in your life. All you can do is rest and recuperate tonight. Perhaps tomorrow you will be able to provide the help needed.

Ten minutes after lying down on the couch, the phone rings. Your friend on the other end of the line explains that someone had to drop out of his or her foursome. They will be teeing off in twenty minutes. The green fees have been paid; can you make it? Amazingly, strength, energy and vitality rush through your being. You grab your clubs and are out the door. How can this be? Simply this: we create enthusiasm for anything we want to create enthusiasm for. Enthusiasm is a choice in the same way that attitude is a choice.

People of impact bring great energy and enthusiasm to everything they put their hands to. They create it! They know that energy is infectious. It is like a magnet. It draws people like nothing else. If you are not enthusiastic, there is no way anyone else will be. You need to leave your problems at home. But you can not afford to leave your home without enthusiasm. Enthusiasm will accomplish what persuasion cannot.

Enthusiasm Is An Attitude

Allan Bellamy is the epitome of enthusiasm. He claims that most people let conditions control their attitudes instead of controlling conditions with their attitudes.

When Allan came home from the Korean War, his mother invited him to join her in a very small "Mom and Pop" type of grocery store. Allan says it was so small that when you opened the front door it bumped against the meat counter, which was at the back door. Business was good—so good that he wasn't bashful about talking to a banker about a loan, a big one, to expand the store. With limited capital but unlimited enthusiasm, he persuaded the bank to lend him enough to build a "super" market. His business grew and prospered for the next six months. Then word leaked out that Pine Bluff, Arkansas, was the place to build a supermarket.

During the next six months, ten major chain competitors opened stores in the area. Every new opening took more of his business. Soon he was doing less business in the big store than he had done in the little store.

Then Bellamy and four of his people signed up for a public speaking course, which placed emphasis on the right mental attitudes. The fifth session was on enthusiasm! After that night, Allan decided that he and his people would be five times as enthusiastic as ever before. His customers were met at the front door with an enthusiastic welcome and the entire workplace attitude, from top to bottom, changed dramatically...as did the results. In just four weeks the business doubled and hasn't fallen back since.

The enthusiasm of the Mad Butcher, Inc. was so contagious that there was virtually no turn-over of employees. Enthusiasm became a way of corporate life, and it led to twenty-six more highly successful stores!

What is enthusiasm? It comes from two Greek words *"en"* and *"theos"* which simply means: "God within!" ***We should all be in the enthusiastic people business! Build your people and your people will build your business!***

136

He who has no fire of enthusiasm in himself cannot light a fire in others.
~RJS~

Rick Olson and Robert Strand have used their speaking, writing, and consulting skills to elevate businesses and organizations across America. To find out more information about them, please call Rick Olson Seminars at 1-800-325-4007 or visit Rick's website, www.rickolsonseminars.com. We would be happy to get you a complete listing of their services and books.

Rick Olson is in great demand as a keynote speaker. He has also focused on staff and management training, as well strategic planning. His themes include: service, sales, management dynamics, team building, handling change, stress reduction, marketing, and work/family balance. In addition, he provides companies monthly newsletter articles on service and stress reduction in the workplace.

Robert Strand's books have inspired millions. As one of America's foremost story tellers, his *Moments* books have become favorites for businesses, associations, and churches to give as gifts. He has also written a number of books that are being used to help move people to a better way of living. Now numbering 47, his books cover a wide range of topics. Robert is a popular convention speaker.